REA

ACPL
DISCARDED

D1031124

320
Cohen, Youssef.
RADICALS, REFORMERS, AND
REACTIONARIES

ALLEN COUNTY PUBLIC LIBRARY
FORT WAYNE, INDIANA 46802

You may return this book to any location of
the Allen County Public Library.

DEMCO

RADICALS REFORMERS AND REACTIONARIES

THE PRISONER'S DILEMMA AND THE COLLAPSE OF DEMOCRACY IN LATIN AMERICA

YOUSSEF COHEN

THE UNIVERSITY OF CHICAGO PRESS
Chicago and London

Allen County Public Library
900 Webster Street
PO Box 2270
Fort Wayne, IN 46801-2270

Youssef Cohen is associate professor in the Department of Politics at New York University.

The University of Chicago Press, Chicago 60637
The University of Chicago Press, Ltd., London
© 1994 by The University of Chicago
All rights reserved. Published 1994
Printed in the United States of America
03 02 01 00 99 98 97 96 95 94 1 2 3 4 5
ISBN: 0-226-11271-3 (cloth)
0-226-11272-1 (paper)

Library of Congress Cataloging-in-Publication Data

Cohen, Youssef.
Radicals, reformers, and reactionaries : the prisoner's dilemma and the collapse of democracy in Latin America / Youssef Cohen.
p. cm.
Includes bibliographical references and index.
1. Latin America—Politics and government—1948– 2. Democracy—Latin America. 3. Prisoner's dilemma game. 4. Brazil—Politics and government—1954–1964. 5. Chile—Politics and government—1970–1973. I. Title.
JL966.C64 1994
320.98′09′045—dc20 93-43274
CIP

∞The paper used in this publication meets the minimum requirements of the American National Standard for Information Sciences—Permanence of Paper for Printed Library Materials, ANSI Z39.48-1984.

To Lindsay and Max

CONTENTS

FIGURES

ACKNOWLEDGMENTS

As I was writing this book, a number of people had to endure my endless obsessive chatter and my long clumsy drafts. For their patience, support, advice, and constructive criticism I am deeply grateful to Barry Ames, Henri Barkey, Karen Barkey, Kirk Beattie, Steven Brams, Brian Brown, Joanne Gowa, Leah Haus, Mark Lilla, Ed Mansfield, Tony Marx, Peter McDonough, Christopher Mitchell, A. F. K. Organski, Franco Pavoncello, Sheldon Pollack, Martin Schain, Nelson do Valle Silva, Amaury de Souza, Maria do Carmo Campello de Souza, Peter Swenson, David Zweig, and the anonymous reader of the manuscript I submitted to the press.

I want to thank John Tryneski, my editor at the University of Chicago Press, for all his support. It was both a pleasure and a privilege to have him as my editor.

I am also grateful to New York University for a Research Challenge Grant, which covered my traveling expenses to Latin America.

1 INTRODUCTION

The sixties and the seventies were two sorry decades for Latin America. Many Latin American countries turned to authoritarianism, including two of its most stable democracies—Brazil and Chile. Each one of these democracies collapsed shortly after its head of state had attempted to implement a wide-ranging program of social reform. In Brazil, Goulart, and in Chile, Allende, had tried to enact a wide set of reforms, ranging from the restructuring of the educational system to the nationalization of foreign enterprises and the expropriation and redistribution of land.[1]

Everybody knows how these experiments in reform ended. Less than three years after legally assuming the presidency Goulart was ousted by the military in 1964.[2] Similarly, within three years of assuming the presidency Allende was removed by the military (and lost his life) in 1973.[3] The causes of the failure of reforms and of the breakdown of democracy in Brazil and Chile and in other South American countries, however, are still a matter of controversy.[4]

The most common explanation is that the severe structural problems typical of contemporary Latin American societies caused the failure of reforms as well as the ultimate collapse of democratic institutions. This structural explanation suggests that, in the sixties and the seventies, the demands for reform, and the democratic arrangements that encouraged them, became incompatible with the requirements of capitalist development in South America.[5] To preserve capitalist growth, reforms and democracy had to be suppressed. Hence the emergence of military regimes. Faced with these structural problems, there was nothing political elites could do to preserve democratic institutions.

The explanation offered in this book is at odds with structural ones. I argue here that structural explanations cannot possibly account for the breakdown of South American democracies in the sixties and the seventies. I shall offer instead an intentional, rational-choice explanation, that is, an explanation based on the preferences and rational choices of the main actors involved in the events that led to that breakdown. In this book I will show that, although structural conditions imposed constraints on their behavior, the actors involved could have chosen alternative courses of action that would have made significant reform possible and would have avoided the dismantling of democratic institutions.

Structural versus Intentional Explanation

The most common causes mentioned in structural explanations are economic ones, involving the nature of Latin American economic development. There are different economic explanations, all of which are variations of the same general argument.[6]

Economic explanations present the emergence of military autocracy as the result of two contradictory aspects of dependent capitalist, or import-substituting, industrialization. On one hand, the exuberant growth of such industrialization in its early stages encourages and absorbs the increasing demands of the lower classes. On the other hand, the inherent limits of such industrialization eventually lead to a drastic decline in the rate of economic growth. To survive, dependent capitalism must therefore generate a military autocracy to contain the rising demands of the lower classes. Thus, the dynamics of dependent development would create, on the one hand, pressures for redistributive reforms, but would also generate, on the other hand, the authoritarian regimes necessary to contain these threatening reforms.

Not all structural explanations are economic ones. A few of these explanations emphasize political factors, such as the overall institutional structure of the polity, the nature of electoral laws, and the structure of the party system.[7] According to these explanations, the political structures typical of Latin American democracies—especially presidentialism, proportional representation, and multiparty systems—are the causes of the political polarization and radicalization that led to the breakdown of democratic institutions in countries like Brazil and Chile.

These economic and political explanations have been the subject of many excellent critiques which found them wanting for a variety of reasons.[8] To some extent, however, the major flaw of these explanations has been insufficiently recognized.[9] The main problem of the usual economic and political explanations of the turn to authoritarianism in Latin America in the sixties and seventies lies precisely in the fact that they are *structural* explanations.[10]

As I will argue in the next chapter, structural explanations often fail because they are based on an inadequate view of the explanatory role of structures.[11] Whereas a given set of structural conditions is normally compatible with several possible outcomes, structural explanations tend to reduce this compatibility to a single outcome. Structural explanations assume that socioeconomic and political structures determine preferences and action, which is to assume that structures can explain political outcomes directly, without reference to intentional phenomena such as values, beliefs, ideas, attitudes, intentions, and strategic thinking. Since class structures, state structures, and the like are seen as causing the individual choices that result in historical outcomes, those societal structures are seen as sufficient to explain these outcomes. Instead of seeing structures as a set of constraints and opportunities for action, structural explanations see them as causing action. As we shall see, this is a self-defeating approach.

Unlike structural explanations, the type of explanation advanced here focuses on the values, beliefs, attitudes, goals, preferences, and strategic calculations of the actors involved in the event to be explained. According to this kind of explanation—which may be properly labeled *intentional*—although values, beliefs, and preferences are conditioned by structures, they can still be largely independent from them.[12] Because beliefs, preferences, and intentions often cannot be inferred from structural conditions, they must be given an autonomous explanatory role.

In all fairness, structural explanations of the breakdown of democracies in South America are not as deterministic as their critics have suggested. Some of their proponents would readily admit that their explanations claim no more than a strong relationship, or an "elective affinity," as Weber would say, between structural variables and the collapse of democracy. Admitting that a particular structural explanation is incomplete, however, is not to admit that all such explanations are bound to be insufficient. Regardless of a scholar's claims concerning the completeness of his explanation of an event, as long as he assumes that its causes are structural, he cannot help but impart inevitability to that event. To make this assumption is to assume that, though still unknown, a set of sufficient structural causes does in fact exist. Of course, if this is the case, then it is possible in principle to predict events without any knowledge of intentional phenomena. Given certain structural conditions, outcomes will follow no matter what the actors involved in these conditions choose to do; there is almost nothing they can do to stop the structures from producing those outcomes.

This book is highly critical of explanations that rely solely on structural variables, even when it is admitted that the explanation is incomplete. For, as we shall see, if this is the case, and the proponent of the explanation makes no effort to deal with intentional phenomena, either he is assuming that structures determine intentions and actions (and that outcomes are inevitable), or he is giving no explanation at all.

Rational Choice, Game Theory, and Democratic Collapse

Explanations that focus on beliefs, values, and intentions may be labeled "intentional" so long as it is understood that this label does not necessarily imply a *direct* causal connection between individual intentions and the final outcome being explained. In dealing with events involving several actors, intentional explanations must incorporate an account of the strategic interaction of those actors. When several actors are involved, the results of their interaction may be unintended by some or all of the protagonists.[13] Wars, revolutions, and military coups are often the unintended consequences of strategic interaction. Nevertheless, we can still speak of an intentional explanation in the sense that those events *ultimately* (or indirectly, via interaction) resulted from the intentions of several actors. A complete intentional explanation will therefore include both a description of the beliefs and goals of actors and an analysis of the strategic interaction that resulted in the outcome being explained.

Rational-choice explanation is a type of intentional explanation, one in which actors choose rationally from a set of available options.[14] Just what it is to "choose rationally" is a fairly complex and subtle matter and will be dealt with in a separate chapter.[15] For now, an informal definition will do: given a set of beliefs, and a set of alternatives, an individual will choose rationally if he chooses the course of action which is the best means to achieve his goals (or satisfy his desires).

From a rational-choice perspective, rational action is the causal mechanism linking structures to the outcome being explained. From this perspective, structural variables cannot directly explain outcomes because, although they affect them, they do not determine preferences and action. Structures and institutions define only a set of constraints and opportunities, that is, a set of possible courses of action. Rational-choice theory is therefore necessary to define the mechanism by which people choose among those alternatives.[16]

When several rational actors are involved, and the outcome is the result of their strategic interaction, rational-choice explanations must rely on game theory. When the achievement of an actor's goal depends on the behavior of others, a rational actor will take into account what others are likely to do before he chooses among alternative courses of action. And he will assume that, being rational, other actors will condition their choices on what he and all the other actors are likely to do.[17] A theory that can tell us how actors mutually condition each other's choices—a theory of strategic interaction—is therefore necessary to the explanation of events involving more than one actor. This is precisely what game theory is about.

Since the breakdown of democracy is explained here as the outcome of the strategic interaction among rational political actors, the type of explanation used in this book is intentional, rational-choice, and game-theoretic.

The Argument in a Nutshell

Structural explanations of the demise of democracy argue that democratic institutions collapsed in Latin America because they had become incompatible with the requirements of capitalist dependent development. Democracy had generated an ever-increasing pressure for redistributive reforms that had clashed with the austerity that capitalist growth required in the fast-developing nations of South America. The redistributive demands of the lower classes had to be suppressed and democracy had to be replaced by military autocracy. The major implication of this structural account is that significant social reforms could not have been enacted within the developing capitalist South American democracies of the sixties and seventies.

My argument runs against this implication. As I intend to argue, the structural conditions prevailing in Latin American countries did not preclude the implementation of substantial socioeconomic and political reforms. In the cases of Brazil and Chile, there was a great deal of support for social reform at the time Goulart and Allende rose to power.[18] And support was by no means confined to the Left. A clear majority among political elites, as well as among the population at large, supported at least a moderate version of the program of reforms that Goulart and Allende proposed at the start of their respective presidential terms.

In principle this moderate majority of reformists could have enacted major socioeconomic and political changes within a democratic framework. Although the majority of moderates was split into a left-leaning and a right-leaning camp that had divergent interests, both sides had strong incentives to cooperate in the passing of a moderate program of reforms. The leftist moderates wanted, of course, a broader set of reforms than the right-leaning ones. But each moderate side had much to gain from cooperating with the other in implementing a moderate program of reforms.

The problem was that each moderate side suspected the other's ultimate intentions. For reasons I will explain in chapter 5, each moderate side had good reason to fear that the other had much to gain from colluding with the extremists in its own camp. Although each moderate side knew that the other stood to gain from an agreement on reforms, each side feared that, if it cooperated, the other side could gain even more by colluding with the extremists to impose its own program of reforms. The moderate right felt that, if it cooperated toward reaching an agreement, the moderate left would join the extreme left to take advantage of its cooperation. Conversely, the moderate left feared that the moderate right would join the extreme right to take advantage of its own cooperation. It was this complex set of relations between radicals, reformists, and reactionaries—rather than economic and political structures—which led to the final confrontation that resulted in the collapse of democratic institutions.

In the language of game theory, the moderates failed to reach an agreement on reforms because they were involved in a prisoner's dilemma game.[19] *Given their set of preferences,* the two moderate camps were caught in the throes of a prisoner's dilemma which precluded an agreement on a program of reforms. Although both moderate sides would have preferred to cooperate in reaching an agreement so as to prevent a confrontation between the left and the right, the logic of the prisoner's dilemma led them into the confrontation they so badly wanted to avoid. In the end, no reforms were implemented and democratic institutions collapsed. Instead of benefiting from the moderate reforms they had wanted, most people found themselves under a military dictatorship they wished they could have avoided.

Plan of the Book

The next two chapters of the book criticize structural explanations, in particular structural explanations of the collapse of democracy. In chapter 2, I explain the logic of structural explanation and of functional explanation, and show how, in the social sciences, both types of explanation have failed to provide us with the causal mechanisms linking structural variables and the outcomes they purport to explain. In this chapter I also show that, even if structural arguments use rational-choice theory to provide such causal mechanisms, structural explanations would still need to explain how structures shape preferences. Since preferences are likely to be largely autonomous from structural conditions, and it has proven to be extremely difficult to derive the former from the latter, I argue that, at least for the near future, it is wiser to include both structural conditions and intentional phenomena in our explanations. Chapter 3 examines current explanations of the demise of democracy in the light of chapter 2, to show that another type of explanation is needed.

In chapter 4, I discuss intentional and rational-choice explanations, and I briefly discuss game theory and the prisoner's dilemma. Chapter 5 presents a game-theoretic explanation of the collapse of democracy. In this chapter, I show that, when the moderates are involved in a prisoner's dilemma game, no agreement on a set of reforms will be reached and the democratic regime will collapse. I then show, in chapters 6 and 7, how the general argument developed in chapter 5 can explain the Chilean and Brazilian cases.

2 STRUCTURAL EXPLANATION

In this chapter I lay out the logic of structural explanation and point out its problems and limitations. Though my argument is critical of structural explanation, it is in no way against the incorporation of structural conditions in the explanation of political phenomena. On the contrary, I assume that any explanation must state the structural conditions defining the set of feasible alternatives for the actors involved. My objections are only to pure structuralists, that is, to those who assume that structural causes are sufficient ones.

On the other hand, I also take issue with the extreme form of methodological individualism adopted by pure individualists, who reduce structures to the actions and interactions of individuals. Instead, I side with those who have argued for a methodological approach that is both structuralist and individualist.[1]

The Logic of Structural Explanation

A full explanation of an outcome requires the following three successive steps. The first step consists of a description of the set of feasible actions for each of the actors involved. Structural conditions enter at this stage of the explanation, for these define what actors can and cannot do to achieve their goals. As Jon Elster puts it, the set of structural constraints "cuts down the set of abstractly possible courses of action and reduces it to the vastly smaller subset of feasible actions."[2]

The second step toward a full explanation consists in defining the mechanism by which one of the alternative feasible actions is selected. In other words, once the feasible options for each actor are listed, one must explain how each actor came to choose one of those options. Finally, the third step of the explanation consists in showing how the choices of the actors led to the outcome being explained. Obviously, when actors mutually condition each other's choices, the second and third steps collapse into one. In this case, it is impossible to explain any actor's choice without simultaneously explaining all of the other actors' choices, and to do so is to show how their choices led to the outcome being explained.

Typically, structural explanations give almost no importance to the last two steps. In these explanations structural constraints are of overwhelming importance, to the point where these constraints dictate action, that is, they leave actors no choice but to act in a single predetermined way. Pushing it to its deterministic extreme, the logic of structural explanation assigns all of the explanatory weight to the set of structural constraints by having them reduce the set of abstractly possible courses of action to a *single* feasible option.[3] According to this logic, actors have no choice and, therefore, their beliefs, preferences, and goals are unimportant in the explanation of the outcome resulting from their actions. All we need to know are the structural constraints under which they act to account for both their actions and the ensuing outcome.

To give an illustration of this logic and its flaws, consider Theda Skocpol's explanation of revolutions.[4] Skocpol rejects "voluntaristic" explanations of revolution, arguing that its causes lie in state and class structures. According to her, the key to social revolutions is to be found in the structural position of the state within the international system, the structural relations between the state and its own domestic classes, and the internal relations between those classes.

Succinctly put, her explanation is as follows. Involved in wars to maintain its position in the world system, the agrarian state was compelled to extract more and more resources from its population. Where the dominant agrarian classes had sufficient power to resist taxation, the coercive capacity of the state was severely weakened. This weakening, in turn, opened the door to peasant rebellions. Squeezed between other powerful states and its own domestic classes, the warring agrarian state collapsed and a revolutionary dynamic ensued.

3 1833 02687 5184

In Skocpol's analytical scheme there is no room for the actual beliefs, preferences, and goals of state managers and of members of the several classes. Everything occurs as if state actors had no choice but to engage in warfare and to extract ever-increasing amounts of resources from the population; as if the agrarian upper classes had no alternative but to resist the state and to pass the burden of taxation onto the peasants, who then had no choice but to rebel.[5] It is as if there was no opportunity for bargaining and compromise, no room for normal politics, only for coercion and extraction. States that were successful in making necessary domestic reforms and in avoiding revolutions are explained in terms of structural conditions; never in terms of the beliefs and preferences of state managers.

This does not mean that Skocpol's explanation is wrong. Although there is a growing literature suggesting that the beliefs and preferences of state managers make a substantial difference to whether revolutions occur or not, Skocpol's conjectures about the effects of class and state structures may still be largely correct.[6] The problem with her explanation is that it is radically incomplete. Rather than demonstrating that structural constraints forced the main protagonists to act in the ways predicted by her theory, she seems merely to assume that they did. In Skocpol's theoretical scheme there is no systematic discussion of the possible courses of action available to key actors, nor is there any discussion of how structural constraints compelled them to act in the way they did. Instead, Skocpol seems to impute interests to actors and to imply that, given the structural situation, they could only act in one way to achieve their goals.

Even though structuralists like Skocpol can sometimes accurately predict an outcome on the basis of structural conditions, their methodological position prevents them from developing satisfactory explanations. Structuralists' refusal to deal with their own implicit assumptions concerning beliefs and preferences prevents them from going beyond mere correlational statements linking structures to outcomes. This refusal is unfortunate, for it can be shown that the arguments of structuralists like Skocpol can be greatly improved precisely by adopting the methodological position she rejects.[7]

Before I show this, however, I must discuss the explanatory

strategy structuralists often use to produce causal statements without referring to intentional phenomena. Unwittingly, structuralists often make illegitimate inferences based on flawed functionalist thinking. From a correlation between a social phenomenon and its alleged effect (function), structuralists often infer that the phenomenon is caused by its effect.[8] In this way, for instance, structuralists have inferred, from a mere correlation between military political repression and economic growth, that military regimes emerge because they are necessary to the maintenance of capitalist structures.

In the remainder of this chapter I will first argue that most functionalist structural explanations in the social sciences are flawed. I will also argue, after Jon Elster, that although this form of explanation can in principle succeed in the social sciences, it is unlikely that its severe requirements can be met in explaining most of the phenomena of interest to social scientists. After discussing this kind of explanation, I will return to nonfunctionalist structural explanations like Skocpol's. The argument here is that, although this latter type of explanation could be improved by explicitly incorporating intentional phenomena and the logic of choice, in doing so one would radically change the nature of the explanation.

Functionalist Structural Explanation

The Logic of Functional Explanation

As Jon Elster has noted, the strong attraction functionalist explanation has for social scientists is probably due to its implicit assumption that social phenomena *must have meaning*.[9] Rather than being a tale told by an idiot, social life takes the forms it takes because these have beneficial consequences for human society. In its extreme version, functionalism assumes that *all* social phenomena have beneficial consequences (functions), and that it is these beneficial consequences that explain those phenomena. The more moderate version of functionalism assumes only that, *whenever* social phenomena have beneficial consequences, these consequences explain them.[10]

It is not that human beings deliberately design social institutions that have beneficial consequences for society. On the contrary, functionalist thinking excludes intentional design. Causality is attributed to impersonal mechanisms that select structures and behaviors that have beneficial consequences. Characteristically, functionalist thinkers assume social processes are guided by a purpose; but there is no purposive actor directing the process.[11] In Hegelian fashion, history is a "process without a subject" and human actors are the unwitting "bearers" of functions assigned to them. The radical alternative to this view is, of course, that history is full of accidents and unintended consequences without meaning—full of sound and fury, signifying nothing.

Functional explanation, then, is characterized by two basic features. In the first place, the causes of social phenomena are their consequences. Social phenomena are explained by their beneficial consequences to someone or something. Conservatives, for instance, often explain social institutions by their beneficial effects to society, whereas radicals tend to explain them by their beneficial effects to a class. Secondly, since history is a process without a subject, the beneficial consequences of the social institutions being explained are neither intended nor recognized by those who benefit from them.[12]

To illustrate the features of a functional explanation, we can use an example offered by Arthur Stinchcombe: Malinowski's explanation of magic among Trobriand islanders.[13] Malinowski observed that, before fishing in dangerous high seas, islanders practiced magic more heavily than when they fished in the safer waters of a lagoon. He concluded that magic was used because it maintained the islanders' conviction that they controlled the outcome of their activities, thereby reducing their anxiety in the face of uncertainty: the greater the uncertainty, the more they engaged in magical appeal to supernatural forces. Malinowski's explanation of magic is obviously functional. He explained magic by its beneficial consequences to the islanders, who did not recognize the true reason for which they engaged in magic. The islanders thought that, by engaging in magic, they were actually increasing the probability of a successful fishing expedition, when in fact they were only reducing their anxiety. According to Malinowski, what explains magic—relief from anxiety—is therefore unintended and unrecognized by the islanders, that is, by those who benefit from it. Rather than explaining magic through the intentions of islanders, Malinowski explains it by its function—to maintain a *conviction* of control over outcomes in the face of danger. Magic did not give them control; it helped them *believe* they had power.

The formal structure of a functional explanation can be graphically represented as in figure 1.

In figure 1, *X* is the structure or behavior that is being explained and *Y* is the beneficial consequence of *X*, which explains the emergence and maintenance of *X*. In the presence of *T*—upsetting tensions that threaten the production of beneficial consequences *Y*—the structure *X* is maintained through the causal loop going from *Y* to *X*. In the case of the Trobriand islanders, for instance, magic is *X*, anxiety level (or degree of conviction of control) is *Y*, and danger (or degree of uncertainty) *T*. As *T* (danger) increases, *Y* (anxiety) increases. The increase in *Y* (anxiety) then triggers a causal mechanism that generates *X* (magic), which, in turn, reduces the level of *Y* (anxiety). This causal mechanism, of course, must specify how the group that benefits from a reduction in *Y* will produce more of *X* without intending or recognizing its true beneficial consequences. In the case of the islanders, specifying a causal mechanism would involve saying exactly how anxiety leads people like the islanders to engage in magic.

Figure 1 The Causal Structure of a Functional Explanation

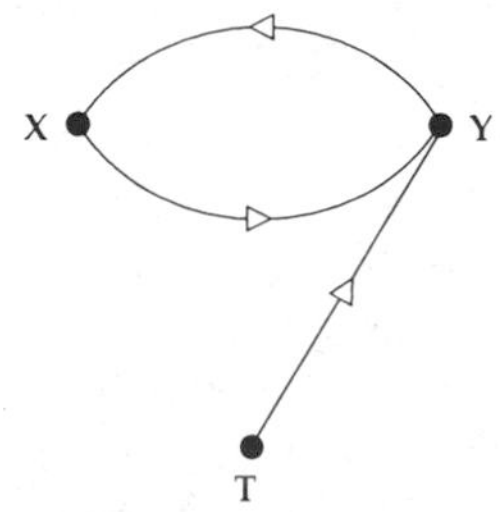

Source: Adapted from Arthur L. Stinchcombe, *Constructing Social Theories* (New York: Harcourt, Brace & World, 1968), p. 89.

Problems of Functionalist Explanations

From the discussion above, it should be evident that one must do more than simply show that *Y* is an effect of *X* to conclude that *Y* (the function of *X*) explains the structure or behavior *X*. To use our example, it is not sufficient to show that there is a correlation between magical activity and the level of anxiety to conclude that the need to reduce anxiety explains magic among the islanders. If it were enough to show such a correlation (between *X* and *Y*), then we would be entitled to make absurd conclusions; for example, from the observation that sunshine helps tomatoes grow, we could conclude that, somehow, tomatoes cause the sun to shine.[14]

Obviously, then, to explain something by its function requires more than showing that *Y* is an effect of *X*. We also need to show how *Y* selects and maintains *X;* that is, we need to specify the *causal mechanism* by which *Y,* the consequence, causes the phenomenon *X* we want to explain. And this is what most attempts at functional explanation fail to do.

Elster gives an instructive example of this failure: Lewis Coser's conjecture about the ossification of bureaucracies. Coser argued that "conflict within and between bureaucracies provides the means for avoiding the ossification and ritualism which threatens their form of organization."[15] The argument suggests that the prevention of ossification *explains* bureaucratic conflict; that is, conflict is explained by its function—the prevention of ossification.

Interpreted this way, Coser's conjecture is an attempt to give a functional explanation of bureaucratic conflict, where *X* is conflict and *Y* the level of ossification. The attempt failed, however, because Coser never went beyond stating that ossification (*Y*) is an effect of conflict (*X*); that is, that ossification and conflict are inversely related. Even if this were true, Coser would still have to specify the causal mechanism that would lead an increase in ossification to spur more conflict. To complete his explanation, Coser would have to tell us precisely how those who benefit from a decrease in ossification, without either recognizing the process or intending it, produce the amount of conflict necessary to prevent ossification and ritualism.[16]

Instead of giving us this causal account, Coser vaguely says that conflict "provides the means" for avoiding ossification, without ever referring to human actors and their intentions. Rather than a valid functional explanation, Coser's conjecture is a failed one that takes the form of an *objective teleology,* a process guided by a goal but without an intentional subject.[17]

Functionalist Structuralism and Objective Teleology

Like Coser's conjecture, structural explanations tend to be incomplete functional explanations that take the form of an objective teleology. Take, for example, Marx's structural explanation of Bonapartism.[18] According to Marx, the Eighteenth Brumaire and the Empire occurred because they were beneficial to capitalism. The general argument, of course, is that noncapitalist states are beneficial to, and therefore explained by, capitalism. Marx argued that noncapitalist forms of government—such as the Empire in France and rule by the aristocracy in England—benefited the capitalist class either because these forms allowed the state to appear as a neutral arbiter between classes or because they generated political struggles that deflected energy from the class struggle.[19]

Marx's explanation is undoubtedly structural. An economic structure, capitalism (*Y*), is the direct cause of a political structure, a noncapitalist government (*X*). However, instead of specifying the causal mechanism linking *Y* to *X,* Marx resorts to a typical, but illegitimate, functionalist maneuver. From the plausible argument that *Y* is an effect of *X*, namely, that the maintenance of capitalism is a beneficial consequence of noncapitalist government, he infers that the former is a cause of the latter. But this does not necessarily follow. It may be that, under certain conditions, the maintenance of capitalism is an *effect* of noncapitalist forms of government, but this does not necessarily mean that capitalist structures *cause* them; their causes could lie elsewhere.

To show that the requirements of capitalism actually are the cause of noncapitalist governments or Bonapartism, Marx should have specified the causal mechanism by which capitalism selects these forms of government when it needs them. Specifying the mechanism would have necessarily involved showing how the members of the capitalist class unintendedly brought about Bonapartism.[20] Yet, as Elster has convincingly argued, Marx's explanation has no explanatory room for either the intentional or the unintentional actions of capitalists.[21] Like Coser's, his argument implies an objective teleology, a process that has a purpose—the maintenance of capitalism through certain political structures—but no purposeful actor.

True, one could complete Marx's explanation by arguing that capitalists deliberately bring about noncapitalist governments. In this case, capitalists would be adopting an indirect strategy: deliberately forfeiting the crown in order to save the purse.[22] But this argument is neither a structural nor a functional explanation. Its logic is, rather, that of an intentional explanation, because the beliefs, perceptions, preferences, and choices of the actors become the central elements of the argument. And this is clearly not the logic of Marx's, or of Marxist and neo-Marxist, theories of the state. These theories tend to explain the forms, structures, and policies of the state as direct effects of the capitalist system, without referring to any human actors, their choices, and their interactions.[23]

Flawed functional explanation and objective teleology pervade not only Marxist theories of the state. Elster has arrayed an impressive amount of examples showing that flawed functionalism is all-pervasive in Marxist history and social science as well. He shows that historians such as E. P. Thompson and John Foster, as well as philosophers and social scientists like Louis Althusser, Nicos Poulantzas, James O'Connor, Samuel Bowles, and Herbert Gintis, among others, have analyzed a wide variety of phenomena (ranging from peasant rebellions and food riots in preindustrial England to education in twentieth-century America) in flawed functional-teleological terms.[24] They all seem to have taken for granted that the requirements of capitalist structures explain everything that occurs in capitalist society, for they have not felt a need to specify the causal mechanisms linking those structures to the phenomena they want to explain. Their structural explanations fail because they are based on incomplete functional explanations, implying unjustifiable objective teleologies.

Elster also shows that Marxists are not alone in misusing functional explanation. A wide variety of non-Marxist social scientists, ranging from Malinowski, Merton, and Coser to Foucault and Bourdieu, also do.[25] But this does not mean that functionalist arguments in the social sciences are doomed to failure. Elster suggests, however, that the small incidence of success of functional explanation in the social sciences may reflect the fact that these sciences cannot invoke a general causal mechanism (equivalent to natural selection in biology), which could in principle justify explaining social phenomena by their beneficial consequences.[26] Social scientists are therefore in the awkward position of having to specify a particular causal mechanism for each phenomenon they study; there can be no general presumption that social phenomena can be explained by their function.

To Elster, all of this indicates that functional explanation can only have a very minor role in the social sciences, and that social scientists should therefore turn to other kinds of explanation, especially to intentional explanation. We need not agree with Elster, of course.[27] But, at a minimum, I believe we must require functional explanations to specify the causal mechanisms through which social phenomena can be explained by their function.[28]

By the same token, we must require functionalist structural explanations to specify the causal mechanisms through which social phenomena can be explained by their beneficial consequences to societal structures. Furthermore, since there is no reason to presume that social phenomena can be explained by their functions, when functionalist structuralists cannot find the causal mechanisms necessary to validate their structural explanations, they should at least try other types of explanation. As we shall see, intentional explanations can often succeed where functionalist structural ones have failed.

Nonfunctionalist Structural Explanation

The nonfunctionalist type of structural explanation is really a rudimentary form of intentional explanation. As I have already argued, structural explanations that do not resort to functionalist arguments only *appear* to be free of the need to include statements about the beliefs, preferences, and intentions of the actors involved. In fact, structural explanations implicitly impute values and interests to those actors.[29] Structuralists sometimes explicitly recognize that the causal impact of structures on social phenomena is mediated by the values and interests of actors. But, even when they do so, structuralists tend to assume that these values and interests are so obvious as not to require any special analysis. The effect of these on the outcome being explained would be too trivial to be scrutinized in any analytical detail.[30]

Though this may sometimes be the case, it is certainly far from always being the case. In many instances, explaining how an actor chose from the set of alternatives allowed by a set of structural constraints is a very complicated affair. Moreover, showing how a collective outcome results from the choices and interactions between several actors is as far from a trivial exercise as one can get. For a long time, for example, structuralists erroneously assumed (and many still do) that people who shared the same interests would spontaneously engage in collective action to protect and promote those interests. This assumption was the basis for explanations of a whole range of forms of collective action, from voting patterns to revolutionary action, because it allowed structuralists to infer such collective outcomes from the structurally defined interests of the actors producing those outcomes. It is now a truism that the "free rider problem" forbids such automatic inferences from individual interests to collective action.[31]

This does not mean that structural explanations will always make the wrong predictions. It only means that, because they neglect the nontrivial ways in which intentional phenomena mediate between structures and outcomes, they run a high risk of doing so. But even when they make the correct predictions, structuralists are relying on unexamined intuitions and incomplete explanations. The fact that their intuition did not lead them astray in predicting an outcome on the basis of a set of structural constraints does not mean that they provided us with a satisfactory explanation. For to answer *why* those structural conditions produced that outcome is to explain why the actors involved in producing that outcome chose to act in the ways they did and how their choices produced the collective action being explained. In other words, to produce satisfactory explanations, nonfunctionalist structuralists have no choice but to resort to intentional forms of explanation.

To illustrate this, let me return to Skocpol's explanation of social revolutions. Skocpol does not resort to functionalist arguments, but her explanation runs into problems typical of nonfunctionalist structural explanations. As I have already noted, the first part of her argument—that which deals with the collapse of old regime states—is problematic because she assumes (instead of demonstrating) that state managers had no choice but to act in the disastrous ways they did.

Even more problematic is the second part of Skocpol's explanation—that which deals with peasant rebellions. According to Skocpol, peasant rebellions play an important role in bringing about social revolutions. Their occurrence is favored by two structural conditions. The collapse of the coercive capacity of the state opens the door to peasant rebellions, while strong *community* relations among the peasants increases the likelihood of successful revolutionary collective action.[32]

Now, aside from some vague remarks about peasant communities forming the social and organizational basis for peasant revolt, Skocpol never elaborates on how the degree of community in peasant villages affects the behavior of peasants. This neglect is probably due to Skocpol's commitment to structuralism, which prevents her from including in her explanation statements involving the motivations of peasants. She therefore stops short of a genuine explanation, offering instead a *correlational* statement linking a structural variable to a form of collective action: the stronger the community the higher the probability of a peasant rebellion.

Ironically, Skocpol's argument can be further developed by resorting to the kind of explanation she openly rejects. Michael Taylor has shown how Skocpol's argument can be improved, and even better defended, by resorting to an intentional type of explanation.[33] He argues that, although Skocpol's argument concerning community and rebellion is essentially correct, her explanation is radically incomplete because she fails to provide "the intervening links showing the effect of social structure on the individuals and the interaction between the individuals"—in this case, the effect of community on individual peasants and their interaction.[34] Taylor goes on to show that strong communities were more likely to generate peasant rebellions because a strong community made it *rational* for a peasant to rebel.[35]

Taylor notes that a strong community facilitates cooperation among peasants, and therefore makes participation rational, "not just because individual behavior can more easily be monitored, but because a strong community has at its disposal an array of powerful, positive and negative social sanctions," sanctions that "can be used as selective incentives, not only to induce individuals simply to contribute or participate, but also to bolster conditional cooperation—which is always a precarious business."[36] In the absence of community, the villager has a much greater incentive *not* to participate in collective action. Since weaker communities do not have the means to punish free riders, or to reward participation, the individual peasant has an incentive to let the others rebel; he will get the benefits of rebellion anyway. As a consequence, no one will have an incentive to rebel and a rebellion will not take place.

Rational-choice theory can thus tell us *why* community favors spontaneous peasant rebellion. The rational-choice theory of collective action tells us why, in strong communities, rebellion becomes a feasible option, and it tells us why, in such communities, a rational peasant (who wants to improve the material conditions of his life) should choose that option. This is much more than what Skocpol's structural explanation (or, better, correlation) can do, and is perfectly compatible with her argument and conclusions. Yet her methodological position would lead her to reject Taylor's intentional rational-choice explanation of peasant rebellions.

As Taylor has noted, Skocpol's (and other structuralists') rejection of intentional explanation seems to be based on a misunderstanding.[37] She rejects "voluntarism," claiming people do not "make" revolutions; these are largely the unintended consequences of people acting under structural circumstances which were not of their choosing. This may be so, but a rejection of voluntarism does not imply a rejection of intentional explanation. Though one may argue that nobody intended to bring about the social revolution one is explaining, to provide a complete explanation, one would still have to show how people's intentions and choices led them to usher in a revolution they had not foreseen. Nonvoluntarist explanations of the unintended consequences of social action must nevertheless rely on the original intentions (that failed to materialize) of the actors involved. If I intend to produce *A* but unintentionally produce *B* instead, an explanation of how *B* came to be has to include a statement about how my original intention, and consequent action, produced the "wrong" outcome.

I therefore conclude that, although statements concerning the structural constraints and opportunities under which actors choose are always necessary, such statements are far from being complete explanations of the social phenomena under scrutiny.[38] So-called structural explanations are either radically incomplete or seriously flawed.

When they do not rely on functional explanations, structural arguments remain radically incomplete. As we saw, without reference to the preferences, intentions, and choices of the actors involved, structural conjectures are at best correlational statements rather than genuine explanations.

When they rely on functional explanations, structuralists usually fail to specify the causal mechanisms showing how the phenomenon under investigation can be explained by its beneficial consequences. Even if they tried to, however, it is not clear that they would succeed. Since there is no general causal mechanism like natural selection in the social sciences, it may well be that functional explanation is largely inappropriate for these sciences.

3 STRUCTURAL EXPLANATIONS OF DEMOCRATIC BREAKDOWN

There are two basic types of structural explanation of the collapse of democratic institutions in Latin America. One of them emphasizes economic structures as the ultimate causes of democratic collapse; the other stresses political structures. I will examine each type in turn, showing that both are flawed. I will also explain why I think future attempts to provide adequate structural explanations of breakdown, both of the functionalist and of the nonfunctionalist variety, are unlikely to succeed.

Economic Explanations

Economic explanations argue that the breakdown of democracy and the emergence of military rule in Latin America was the result of the structural contradictions of dependent capitalist, or import-substituting, industrialization. On the one hand, the initial success of such industrialization both encouraged and absorbed the increasing demands of the lower classes. On the other hand, the inherent limits of such industrialization eventually led to a drastic decline in the rate of economic growth. Therefore, to maintain itself, dependent capitalism had to generate a military autocracy to contain the demands of the lower classes.[1] According to economic explanations, that is what happened, for instance, in the countries of the southern cone of Latin America. The economic recession experienced by these countries in the sixties and early seventies is attributed to a crisis of import-substituting industrialization, and this crisis is seen as the cause of the emergence of a military regime. There are three basic variations of this argument.

One group of authors, among them Fernando Henrique Cardoso, Celso Furtado, and Rui Mauro Marini, saw the causes of the economic crisis in the prevailing *distribution of income.*[2] These analysts argued that the slowdown of the economy was caused by the limits imposed on the size of the market for consumer durables and luxury goods by the prevailing distribution of income. According to these authors, dependent capitalist economies grow mainly by substituting for imports of such goods. Since none but the middle and upper classes can acquire goods such as automobiles, growth can proceed only if the increase in income is channeled to those classes at the expense of workers. The solution to the crisis was therefore a further concentration of income in the hands of the upper classes. Because the exuberant growth of the easy phase of import substitution had fostered an increase in the power of workers to make demands as well as in the volume of demands itself, the solution to the crisis required the coercive hand of the military.

A second conjecture is the one proposed by Guillermo O'Donnell.[3] For him, the decline in growth was caused by the *difficulty of deepening* the economy—that is, of substituting for imports of capital goods and achieving a vertical integration of the economic structure. The early, easier phase of substituting for consumer goods had been exhausted, and the resumption of growth through a deepening of the economy required new investments of a size and a period of maturation, as well as a level of technological sophistication, that were far beyond the capacity of the national firms of dependent countries. This meant that the deepening of the economy had to be carried out mainly by the state and multinational corporations. In order to muster the enormous resources needed for such a long-term project and to attract foreign capital, however, the level of consumption and the political activity of the working class had to be contained. Since the working class had been permitted to organize during the previous period of economic growth and democracy, its demands were on the rise, and the military regime was necessary to secure the compliance of workers.

The third argument concerning the relation between economic crisis and the breakdown of democracy is centered around runaway inflation and a balance-of-payments crisis. Albert Hirschman, Thomas Skidmore, and others have suggested that the economic crisis of the sixties in South American countries was due to a *decline in the effectiveness of the unorthodox policies* pursued at the beginning of import-substituting industrialization—a decline that exacerbated inflation and the shortage of foreign exchange.[4] This unorthodox policy package consisted of using an overvalued exchange rate, in combination with import controls, in order to favor domestic industry at the expense of the export sector. Obviously, this combination cheapened imports of machinery and other materials essential to industry, which were given preferential status by the government. The overvalued rate thus favored new industries while decreasing the real income of traditional exporters. In the end, this unorthodox policy package was in fact a shrewd mechanism by which income could be transferred from the traditional export sector to the new industries, albeit at the cost of some inflation.[5]

Eventually, however, unorthodox policies became dysfunctional. As traditional exports lost ground, the overvalued exchange rate aggravated the recurrent disequilibrium of the balance of payments. In turn, the import constraints imposed by the shortage in foreign exchange inhibited further growth because import-substituting industrialization is an import-intensive process. Moreover, inflation ran wildly out of control, mainly because of the abuse of unorthodox measures by policymakers and the profligacy of politicians. Foreign capital consequently became much scarcer. Thus, unorthodox policies had a negative impact on growth by aggravating inflation and the shortage of foreign exchange.[6]

The resumption of growth therefore required an improvement in the balance of payments. Since imports could not be reduced without jeopardizing growth, it was necessary to promote exports and encourage the inflow of foreign capital. Both of these strategies required a devaluation of the currency, the dismantling of exchange controls, and stabilization policies to check the disrupting effects of inflation.[7] Such a transition to orthodoxy obviously would hurt many interests—most of all those of the workers, by creating unemployment and keeping wages low.[8] Hence the need for a military regime.

All three economic explanations have been criticized for failing to fit one or another of the Latin American cases they are purported to explain. The first explanation, for instance, which argues that dependent development could no longer proceed without an increase in the concentration of income, cannot account for the Brazilian case. Morley and Smith have shown that the effect of income concentration on economic growth was negligible in Brazil.[9] Moreover, as José Serra has pointed out, to stimulate the consumption of consumer durables it was not necessary to concentrate income; at the time, Brazilian workers were spending more than one-third of their income on such goods.[10] Even if further concentration of income had been necessary, however, it is not clear why a military regime was needed. As Hirschman has noted, much growth in consumer-durable industries has occurred in the total absence of authoritarianism.[11]

O'Donnell's argument is not supported by the evidence either. Perhaps with the exception of Argentina, the difficulties of deepening the economy cannot account for the breakdown of democracy and the rise of authoritarianism in the Southern cone of Latin America. As Robert Kaufman and José Serra have shown, the substitution for imported capital goods, or "deepening," decreased rather than increased during the years that followed the establishment of military regimes, or had nothing at all to do with the establishment of those regimes.[12] If deepening had anything to do with the recession, it was its cause rather than its cure.

It should also be noted that, at least in the Brazilian case, the coup makers themselves thought that growth depended neither on an increased degree of income concentration nor on a deepening of the economy. They did not pursue a growth strategy based on concentration, and they sought to *un*deepen rather than to deepen the economy because they believed that deepening had already been carried too far.[13] The concentration of income that did in fact occur after the military coup was more an unintended than a planned result of the actions of the policymakers of the military regime.[14]

As to the third conjecture, it is also doubtful that the economic crisis was due to rampant inflation and a disequilibrium in the balance of payments. Michael Wallerstein and Werner Baer have presented some evidence showing that the decline in growth generated or greatly accentuated the disequilibrium in the balance of payments and the severe inflation of the sixties, rather than the reverse.[15] It is also doubtful that a military regime was necessary to effect a transition to economic orthodoxy. As Hirschman has pointed out, both in pre-Allende Chile and in Colombia, orthodox policies were implemented without the assistance of a military regime.[16] During the Frei administration, mini-devaluations and export subsidies brought the exchange rate to a more realistic level. Similarly, in Colombia, "subsidies and later mini-devaluations have successfully promoted new agricultural and industrial exports; the average level of protection has been lowered; interest rates have been raised substantially, so that the bulk of credit transactions no longer takes place at negative real interest rates; and a substantial income tax reform has been enacted," all of which took place without the rise of an authoritarian regime.[17]

Economic Explanations as Functionalist Structural Explanations

It can readily be seen that both the economic explanations of the breakdown of democracy and their criticisms focus on the nature of the economic crisis which allegedly led to the emergence of an authoritarian regime. There is no dispute as to the idea that the crisis was caused by economic problems associated with dependent capitalist structures; the disagreement centers around which *specific* set of structural problems led to the economic crisis. And, apparently, no such set has been found that can explain the majority of the cases.

But even if the structural causes of the crisis were pinpointed, the resulting economic explanation would still be radically incomplete. What seems to have escaped the attention of most researchers is the need to specify the essential causal link between the economic crisis and the onset of authoritarianism. If one explains the collapse of democracy as resulting from a structural crisis, then one's main focus should be on *how* the crisis produced that collapse. Economic explanations, however, have little to say about this question. Instead, such explanations seem to rely either on functionalist arguments or on nonfunctionalist imputations of interests.

On a functionalist reading, economic arguments explain the collapse of democracy and the rise of an authoritarian regime by the *function* of such a regime. Military regimes, it is argued, replace democratic ones because they can better maintain the functioning of the structures of dependent capitalist economies. In other words, authoritarianism is explained by its beneficial consequences (function) for the economic structure of dependent capitalism. By allowing dependent development, or import-substituting industrialization, to overcome severe obstacles, authoritarian regimes would maintain dependent capitalist economies. Hence, it is concluded that, when under stress, the economic structures of dependency generate the authoritarian regime that will save them. The consequences of authoritarianism—the maintenance of structures of dependency—become its causes.

For example, consider the conjecture explaining the emergence of authoritarianism as a result of a need for a greater concentration of income. This increase in concentration would be necessary to maintain economic growth, which depends on the domestic production of consumer durables and luxury goods. In this case, authoritarianism is explained by its consequences for the growth, and maintenance, of the dependent economy: an authoritarian regime emerges *because* it is needed to perform a function—concentrate income—which maintains dependent capitalist structures.

The problem with this explanation, however, lies in its silence about the causal mechanism by which the threatened economic structures of dependent capitalism generate the authoritarian regime that will save them. Without a specification of this causal mechanism, the explanation runs into trouble. Without it there is no reason to presume that, just because an authoritarian regime has beneficial consequences for dependent economic structures, these cause the emergence of that regime.

As Hirschman has perceptively noted, authoritarian regimes have in effect led to a concentration of income, but there is no evidence indicating that a need for such concentration caused the emergence of authoritarianism. But Hirschman did not note that the proponents of this explanation were implicitly resorting to a flawed functional argument, by erroneously inferring a causal relation between income concentration and authoritarianism from a mere correlation between these two variables. Not that this inference is in principle unjustifiable; but it can be justified only by providing the causal mechanism describing how the need to concentrate income brings about an authoritarian regime. And this mechanism is not provided by the explanation in question.

The same is true of the other economic explanations. This can be seen by analyzing the general functional logic of economic explanations with the help of figure 1. The structure to be explained (*X*) is the authoritarian regime; the effect, function, or beneficial consequence of this regime (*Y*) is the maintenance of another structure, the dependent capitalist economy; and the tensions that disturb this structure (*T*) are defined differently, depending on the specific economic explanation one adopts. According to all economic explanations, in the presence of these tensions (however defined), dependent capitalism will cause, or reinforce, an authoritarian regime through a causal feedback loop going from *Y* to *X*. Or, to put it another way, disturbed by certain tensions, dependent capitalism will maintain itself by generating an authoritarian political structure.

Economic explanations differ only in the definition of the tensions involved (difficulties with income distribution, with deepening, or with orthodox economic policies). Their flaw is the same—none of them specifies the causal mechanism implied by the feedback loop going from *Y* to *X*, that is, from the maintenance of dependent capitalism to the authoritarian regime. None of the economic arguments provides a precise account of how the tensions of dependent development move the several actors involved to act, and interact, in such a way as to establish the authoritarian regime allegedly necessary to overcome those tensions.

Nor is it likely that a functional explanation will ever succeed in explaining the breakdown of democratic regimes. As we saw, a functional explanation requires the actors who bring about the beneficial consequences, and those who benefit from them, to do so unintentionally.[18] A successful functional explanation of the emergence of a military regime would have to show that the military established the regime with no intention of maintaining dependent capitalist structures; it would also have to show that the capitalists, who would benefit from the regime, were not aware of the causal connection between an authoritarian regime and the maintenance of a dependent capitalist economy. This is clearly impossible. As everyone knows, in most instances of breakdown, both the military and the capitalists justify the establishment of a military regime as necessary to the struggle against communism.[19]

Economic Explanations as Nonfunctionalist Structural Explanations

Defenders of economic conjectures might protest against the functionalist reading of these explanations. They could argue that, in spite of some functionalist overtones, economic explanations do not really mean to explain the emergence of authoritarian regimes by their function. This nonfunctionalist reading would posit a simple causal connection going from the tensions and contradictions of dependent capitalist economies to the breakdown of democracy and the emergence of a military regime.

The causal link between the economic structure and the authoritarian regime would be given by class interests and the class struggle. According to the nonfunctionalist reading, in establishing an authoritarian regime, the military were acting in both their own interests and those of the dominant classes. These classes, who were allied to international capital, had an interest in maintaining dependent capitalism against the onslaught of an increasingly powerful working class. As O'Donnell has put it, "Most propertied Argentine and Brazilian sectors agreed that the popular sector's demands were excessive (both in terms of consumption and power participation), and that capital accumulation would be impossible if those demands were not tightly controlled."[20] Since the exuberant growth of the early phase of import-substituting industrialization had allowed workers to accumulate a substantial amount of power, "most of the propertied sectors [were led] to perceive popular political demands as serious threats to the survival of the existing social arrangements—particularly the class structure, the power distribution, and the international alignments of the countries."[21] Hence the authoritarian regime.

The problem with this kind of explanation lies in its positing a far greater degree of class unity than was the case. As I will show in detail in the three final chapters of this book, all of the groups mentioned in O'Donnell's explanation—the propertied classes, the working classes, and the military—were deeply divided where the definition of their interests was concerned.[22] Shortly before the military coup, a majority among the propertied classes was in favor of implementing social reforms within a democratic framework. The same is true of the working class.

Most of its leaders and representatives were moderate; they were willing to negotiate for a moderate program of reforms. Only the minorities at the extreme right and left argued for radical solutions to social problems. As for the military, until the very last month before the coup most of them were reluctant to establish an authoritarian regime.[23]

In the case of Brazil, for example, Thomas Skidmore and Argelina Figueiredo have provided a great deal of evidence showing there was a majority among both the dominant classes and workers that preferred a moderate solution to the problem of social reform.[24] As a matter of fact, the largest parties of the dominant classes and of the working classes (the PSD and the PTB) engaged in negotiations to pass a moderate program of redistributive reforms. As we shall see, these negotiations could have been successful, but they broke down shortly before the coup of 1964. The radical minorities—within the upper-class UDN and among the variety of groups of the radical left—struggled continually to sabotage the negotiations and radicalize the situation. They eventually succeeded, largely because of major weaknesses in the relations between the groups at the center. Similarly, studies of the collapse of democracy in Chile by Paul Sigmund and Arturo Valenzuela have shown that the fall of Allende was largely due to factional struggles within the main groups involved in the conflicts preceding the breakdown.[25] It is this complicated dynamic (which I will analyze in greater detail in chapter 5)—a dynamic involving political splits within classes as much as those between classes—that eventually led to the emergence of an authoritarian regime.

These crucial within-class and within-group divisions pose a serious problem for structural explanations of democratic collapse. As we saw, structural explanations tend to attribute structural interests to the actors involved: structures define objective interests which determine how actors are to act. This may be so, but when actors, like the members of social classes, who are supposed to have the same objective interests perceive their interests in different ways, structural explanations do not work.

As far as I can see, structural explanations of the breakdown of democracy have been unable to deal with the major divisions within the propertied classes, the popular sector and the military. Since such divisions are essential to the explanation of democratic collapse, a successful explanation must perforce refer to the beliefs, preferences, and goals of the members of the major factions involved as well as the complex interactions among those factions; an intentional explanation is needed.

Political Explanations

Political explanations usually begin by pointing out that, although the economic crisis was certainly an important cause of democratic collapse, it cannot alone account for that event. Had political institutions—especially the structure of the party system—been sturdier, the whole democratic system would not have collapsed. Thus, according to political explanations, the weaknesses of the party systems of Latin American countries were, along with the structural problems of their economies, a major cause of the breakdown of the sixties and early seventies.

Alfred Stepan proposed one of the first systematic arguments along these lines.[26] According to Stepan, the inability of the Brazilian party system to convert the increasing demands for change into powerfully supported programs of reform played an important role in the collapse of the Brazilian democratic system in 1964. Stepan argued that, in the early sixties, the Brazilian party system had lost its major source of aggregation of interests, namely, the uneasy alliance between the labor leaders of the PTB and the businessmen and rural bosses of the PSD, which had been forged by Vargas in 1945. By 1962, "the growing radicalization (both left and right) within the Brazilian polity and the differential attitudes of the PTB and PSD toward industrial strike and especially agrarian reform . . . increasingly fragmented this major source of aggregation."[27] As a result, it was impossible to garner sufficient support either for policies that could remedy the economic problems or for a broader program of sorely needed reforms. Thus the need for the military to intervene.

This kind of argument was developed into a full-blown explanation of democratic breakdown by Juan Linz and Arturo Valenzuela, who applied it to the Chilean case, and especially by Wanderley Guilherme dos Santos, who applied it to the Brazilian case.[28] These authors based their explanations on Giovanni Sartori's model of "polarized pluralism," arguing that the extreme polarization of the Brazilian and Chilean party systems was a major factor causing the establishment of an authoritarian regime in those countries.[29]

Polarized pluralism is a type of multiparty system which is prone to breakdown. Unlike two-party systems, polarized pluralism is a system with a center (one party or a group of parties) which faces the opposition of extreme antisystem parties. These antisystem parties are located at opposite ends of the ideological spectrum, and they systematically attempt to undermine the legitimacy of the regime they oppose. Obviously, this polarized system is characterized by bilateral oppositions, oppositions which are "mutually exclusive: they cannot join forces."[30] Whereas in systems where opposition is unilateral the opposing parties can join forces and propose themselves as an alternative party, in polarized systems the opposition is divided into two irreconcilable camps. This means that polarized systems will be driven by a centrifugal dynamic with a center facing both a left and a right.

Whereas moderate pluralism is governed by a dynamic that drives all parties toward the center and is characterized by moderation, pragmatism, and compromise, polarized pluralism is governed by a dynamic that induces a continual flight from the center and is characterized by ideological extremism and a lack of compromise. In such a system, all parties tend to behave irresponsibly, to promise what they cannot possibly deliver. The center parties behave semi-responsibly because they are likely to govern indefinitely, and the antisystem parties behave irresponsibly because they do not expect to govern. As a result, competition will be characterized by incessant escalation—by what Sartori calls the "politics of outbidding"—where parties "overpromise" in order to bid support away from each other.

Obviously, polarized pluralism, with its centrifugal drives, irresponsible opposition, and unfair competition, has a very high potential for breakdown. As Sartori has noted, such a system of extreme ideological politics "is conducive either to sheer paralysis or to a disorderly sequence of ill-calculated reforms that end in failure." It is not necessarily doomed to failure, but it is "hardly in a position to cope with explosive or exogenous crises."[31]

The postwar Chilean party system was clearly a case of polarized pluralism. As Arturo Valenzuela has shown, the empirical evidence available to us indicates that, from the fifties to the collapse of democracy in the early seventies, Chile had a highly polarized party system.[32] A large proportion of the electorate identified with parties at the extreme of the political spectrum. A survey conducted in Santiago in 1958 revealed that over 55 percent of the respondents classified themselves either as rightists or leftists, while only about 18 percent placed themselves at the center of the ideological spectrum. More recent survey data and electoral results show that these proportions have remained remarkably stable from 1958 to 1970.

According to Valenzuela, this polarization of the Chilean party system precluded the formation of viable centrist movements, which in the end greatly contributed to the breakdown of the democratic regime. As is the case with Sartori's model of polarized pluralism, rather than being genuine centrist movements, the centrist coalitions that were formed in postwar Chile were unstable amalgamations of fragments from the left and the right. This fragility of the center and the consequent inviability of a centrist consensus made the Chilean political system prone to the kind of crisis that occurred during the Allende years, which resulted in the breakdown of the regime. As Valenzuela puts it:

> Sartori's analysis is extremely helpful in understanding the Chilean case, because it explains the repeated surge of centrist movements in Chilean politics which rose at the expense of both Right and Left. Since these centrist movements only minimally represented a viable centrist tendency and were in fact primarily reflections of the erosion of the two extreme poles, they have crumbled, only to make way for a new centrist coalition. The instability of centrist movements, in turn, contributed to difficulties in structuring common public policies because of the resulting fragility of centrist consensus at the decision-making level. The erosion of centrist consensus would accelerate dramatically during the Allende years and contribute directly to the crisis culminating in regime breakdown.[33]

In contrast to the Chilean, the Brazilian party system was far less polarized. Brazil had a party system that was largely clientelistic, with parties that had little ideological coherence.[34] Most of the electorate did not identify with parties along ideological lines, nor did most parties mobilize and organize voters along such lines. Nevertheless, the Brazilian party system became more polarized as the fifties wore on, moving toward full-blown polarized pluralism in the early sixties.

Wanderley Guilherme dos Santos has shown, with remarkable detail, that the Brazilian political system moved from moderate to polarized pluralism in the early sixties.[35] Parties radicalized and the party system polarized, fragmenting itself into equally powerful camps, all of which resulted in a high degree of coalitional instability and a stalemated Congress. Congress either formed momentary veto coalitions or failed altogether to reach relevant decisions concerning the crisis of the sixties and the issues of social reform. To break the stalemate, the president resorted to reshuffling the cabinet, on one hand, and to pressuring Congress from the outside, on the other. Far from solving the crisis, reshuffling accentuated administrative chaos and decisional paralysis, while pressuring Congress aggravated the polarization of the system. Eventually, according to Santos, acute decisional paralysis led to the establishment of a military regime.

Valenzuela's and Santos's explanation of the breakdown of democracy, though plausible, is problematic. As Sartori himself has noted, polarized pluralism often does not culminate in breakdown.[36] The third and fourth French republics and Italy after 1945 are some of the most notable examples of extreme multiparty systems which resisted breakdown. If this is the case, then Valenzuela and Santos should have provided the causal mechanism by which polarized pluralism and decisional paralysis prompted the emergence of authoritarianism.

In the absence of such a mechanism, the explanation of breakdown as resulting from a perverse dynamic of multiparty systems can be interpreted as a flawed functional explanation. According to such an explanation, authoritarian regimes would be explained by their function (beneficial consequences) for political systems under severe stress. Polarized, the multiparty system would no longer adequately perform its function of aggregating interests, ultimately leading the political system into decisional paralysis. An authoritarian regime, therefore, would be needed to make the decisions that multiparty democracy could no longer make.

Thus interpreted, however, the explanation does not work.

For, as we saw, in such a functional explanation the actors who bring about the authoritarian regime would have to do so with no intention of bringing about its beneficial consequences for the political system, that is, of freeing it from decisional paralysis. And we know that this was not the case: the military and civilians who established military regimes in Latin America usually claimed they had to intervene because, among other reasons, the party system was incapable of functioning effectively enough to overcome the reigning crisis. Thus, even if scholars like Santos had attempted to provide a causal mechanism that could justify a functional argument, they would not have been successful.

On the other hand, a nonfunctional version of the explanation linking polarized pluralism to authoritarianism does not work either. I cannot see how a causal connection between the structure of the party system and the emergence of an authoritarian regime can be made without reference to the beliefs and goals of the actors involved. The multiparty system polarized, and Latin American democracies collapsed, ultimately because groups of the left and the right *chose* to take a radical course of action. As Santos himself, and others, have recognized, it was only in the early sixties, when groups of the left and the right had decided to radicalize, that more permanent military regimes appeared in South America.[37] Their radicalization, however, cannot be explained solely by the structure of the party system. There is no reason to assume that the multiparty system left them no choice but to radicalize. And, even if it left them none, structural explanations do not specify the causal mechanism which made it so. They do not specify any such mechanism by which political structures would have compelled some groups of the left and the right to take a radical course of action.

As far as I can see, it is impossible to fully explain the radicalization of either the right or the left (or, for that matter, the political divisions of the center) by reference to either the socioeconomic or the political structure of the Latin American democracies that collapsed in the sixties and seventies. Although the structural situation certainly influenced leaders and groups of the left and the right, structural conditions cannot account for the ideological differences between those who remained moderate and those who chose to radicalize. Radicalization is a choice, and as such it cannot be explained without reference to the beliefs, preferences, and goals of those who make such a choice. The intentions of the actors who were involved in the breakdown must therefore be treated as *largely autonomous from the structural situation,* if we are to understand how structural problems, both political and economic, ultimately culminate in the breakdown of democratic regimes.[38]

4 RATIONAL-CHOICE EXPLANATION

In the next chapter, I offer a rational-choice explanation of the breakdown of democracy. The present chapter lays the foundations for such an explanation. It discusses the general characteristics of rational action and of rational-choice explanations. Since rational-choice explanation is a special type of intentional explanation, I will begin by describing the logic of the latter. I will then discuss the economic model of rationality on which my explanation is constructed, as well as the general structure of rational-choice explanations based on that model. The chapter ends with a discussion of the aspects of strategic rationality, game theory, and the prisoner's dilemma which are directly relevant to this book.

The Structure of Intentional Explanations

Intentional behavior is behavior engaged in for a reason, that is, to bring about some goal. To offer an intentional explanation of an action is to show not only that there were reasons for that action but also that those reasons actually caused it. Otherwise, we would have to count behavior caused by reasons unknown to an actor as intentional action. If I act compulsively, moved by forces I am only dimly aware of, then I can hardly be said to have acted intentionally. This would be the case even if I offered reasons justifying my compulsive behavior.

Reasons for one's actions are defined by one's beliefs and desires (preferences). Given certain beliefs about the nature of the world and the relations between means and ends, one chooses to act in such a way as to realize one's desires. Intentional explanation, then, is a type of explanation in which beliefs and desires (reasons) are the causes of actions. As Jon Elster puts it, intentional explanation "essentially involves *a triadic relation between action, desire and belief*."[1]

A successful intentional explanation of a given behavior must satisfy the following three requirements.[2] In the first place, it must show that, given the actor's beliefs, his behavior was a means of achieving his desires. Second, an intentional explanation must show that the reasons (beliefs and desires) for that behavior caused it.[3] This clause is needed to rule out cases in which an actor's behavior is caused by something other than the reasons he has for acting in the way he did—as is often the case with compulsive behavior.

A third, more subtle, requirement is that the reasons causing the behavior in question cause it "in the right way." This requirement is necessary to exclude cases in which the causal chain from reasons to behavior to the final objective is of the wrong kind. An example of this is the man who shoots another with the intention of killing him and misses, but the shot provokes a stampede of wild pigs that trample the intended victim to death.[4] Obviously, in this case it could not be said that the man killed the victim intentionally.

A final comment on intentional explanation is in order. Intentional explanation is directed to the future: in explaining an action intentionally we must refer to the future state it was intended to generate. This does not mean, however, that intentional explanation explains an action in terms of the future state it was intended to bring about. This would be clearly impossible, for the future cannot explain the present—only intentions concerning the future can. In addition, the intended future state, of course, may never be realized; and some intentions may be inherently unrealizable.

Intentionality and Rationality

Intentional behavior is not necessarily rational. Rational action is usually defined as optimizing behavior. To say that an intentional action was also rational is to show that the actor not only chose one of the possible means to realize his desire but also that he chose the best means of doing so. For this kind of choice to be at all possible, the actor must have *consistent* beliefs and preferences: his beliefs and preferences must not involve logical contradictions and his preferences must be transitive.[5]

When an actor holds contradictory beliefs, he cannot reason because anything may follow from his beliefs. Similarly, when an actor holds inconsistent preferences he cannot really choose because any option may follow from his preferences.[6] Therefore, if an actor holds inconsistent beliefs and preferences he cannot behave rationally and we cannot invoke a rational-choice explanation to explain his behavior. Nevertheless, his behavior can still be intentional.

To show that action can be intentional yet irrational, consider the following example.[7] Suppose a man believes praying will not cure him from disease. Suppose further that, upon contracting a serious disease, he prays because he believes that prayer may help even those who do not believe in prayer. Obviously, he cannot hold both beliefs without running into a contradiction, for this would imply that he believes praying both helps and does not help him. So his decision to pray is irrational, yet it can be intentionally explained.

Irrational action can also stem from inconsistent preferences. Elster has examined a variety of common behaviors that result from such inconsistency.[8] He argues that people normally fall victim to inherently unrealizable desires. Willing myself to sleep, for instance, is an inherently unrealizable desire. It involves a contradiction between the desire to fall asleep and the wish to do so by forcing oneself to sleep. As any insomniac knows, trying to force oneself to sleep is a self-defeating form of behavior; its effect is usually opposite to the goal it was intended to bring about. This is also true of forgetfulness, indifference, belief, love, spontaneity, and courage, which cannot be achieved at will. Anyone deliberately attempting to bring about these states could hardly be said to be rational.

Rational Behavior in Economics

In economic theory the rational actor chooses the alternative that maximizes his expected utility.[9] Given a set of opportunities (available alternatives) and his set of preferences, a rational actor will choose the alternative which yields the greatest value to him, that is, the alternative which maximizes his expected utility.

People who choose in this way act in conformance to the requirements for rational, maximizing, behavior.[10] When *no risk* is involved—when the actor can predict with certainty the outcome of any action he may take—those requirements are that the actor's set of beliefs and preferences be free from contradiction and that his preferences be transitive. We have already discussed the first requirement. As for transitivity, it means that if, for instance, an actor prefers *a* to *b*, and *b* to *c*, he must also prefer *a* to *c*. It is easy to see why this requirement is necessary, for it would be hardly rational to prefer $400 to $300 and $300 to $200, and also prefer $200 to $400. Few would make this mistake, of course, but when the issues are subtle and complex, preferences can easily be intransitive.

As I already argued, these requirements involving the consistency of beliefs and preferences are absolutely necessary to rational, maximizing, behavior. An individual that has inconsistent beliefs or preferences cannot reason and therefore cannot maximize value.

When risk *is* involved in decision-making, and the actor has to deal with the probability of the outcomes of the action he may take, rationality entails conformity to further requirements.[11] Since in this case maximizing utility involves weighting the value of outcomes by the respective probabilities that they will occur, to make a rational choice the actor has to conform to the axioms of probability theory.

Although the rational-behavior model of economic theory is well suited to the purposes of this book, a few words should be said about its limitations.

Some authors have criticized the economic model for being too "thin," that is, for being silent about the formation and nature of beliefs and preferences.[12] The economic model does not require that beliefs and preferences themselves be rational. In that model, beliefs and preferences need not have been formed through rational deliberation, nor do they have to correspond to events and states in the real world. If I believe that sticking pins into dolls will harm my enemies, I would still be rational according to the economic model as long as I act consistently with that belief.

For the critics of the economic model, this is clearly unacceptable. To them, rational behavior must be based on rational beliefs and preferences. According to this broader theory of rationality, in addition to being internally consistent, beliefs and preferences must be formed in a rational way.[13]

To be rational, a belief must be the result of deliberation based on the available evidence. It need not be true, only plausible given the evidence.[14] Rational belief-formation depends not only on processing information adequately but also on collecting it in sufficient amounts. It is obviously difficult to establish optimal criteria for the collection of information. This difficulty makes it always possible to argue that the belief under consideration is rational because it would have been too costly to collect more information. Nevertheless, in many cases it is still possible to say that someone clearly did not collect enough information (or clearly collected too much of it).

By these criteria, one can say that an instance of irrational belief-formation occurs when either strong emotion or a faulty cognitive process prevents one from collecting and processing information in an adequate way.[15] In the first case, powerful feelings and desires can cause one to process evidence incorrectly, resulting in wishful thinking, as in the case of a man whose sexual desire makes him lower his estimate of the probability of contracting a sexually transmitted disease.[16]

Irrational beliefs need not have emotional sources. The mind is normally subject to cognitive illusions that are hard to avoid.[17] The results of many experiments indicate that we make a variety of systematic inferential mistakes which have little to do with our feelings and wishes. For example, people tend to make inferences about the likelihood of events based on personal experience and current events, neglecting impersonal sources of information and past events.[18]

In the presidential campaign of 1972, for instance, trained reporters attached excessive importance to their personal experience of the wildly enthusiastic crowds supporting McGovern.[19] As a consequence, they grossly underestimated the margin by which the senator would lose. The reporters covering McGovern unanimously predicted he could not lose the election by more than ten points, in spite of the fact that they knew all the polls showed he was trailing by twenty points and that no major poll had been wrong by more than 3 percent in the past twenty-four years.

Unlike irrational beliefs, irrational desires and preferences are a far more controversial matter.[20] Nevertheless, it makes sense to say that when powerful unconscious processes distort one's true preferences, those preferences are irrational. The most important example of irrational desire consists in adapting one's preferences to what seems possible. In this case—as the fox did in the famous fable—a person will unwittingly undervalue what he cannot get, as some people do, for instance, when they undervalue a job or a promotion they are unlikely to obtain.[21]

A second criticism of the rational-choice approach as it is often practiced by neoclassical economists is that it is too narrowly focused on individuals. Recently, a number of rational-choice theorists have criticized neoclassical economics and most public choice theories for ignoring, neglecting, or misunderstanding the effect of structures and institutions in shaping individual choice and action. These critics have shown that a rational-choice approach need not be narrowly committed to methodological individualism. They advocate instead a rational-choice approach that is both methodologically individualist and structuralist in the sense that it can and should take into account the effects of societal structures, institutions, organizations, and rules of the game in explaining the choices, actions, and interactions of individual actors.[22]

The rational-choice approach followed in this book incorporates these criticisms of the economic model of rational behavior. Although I accept the basic premises of the economic model, my approach includes the effects of socioeconomic and political structures. But, unlike structuralists, I see such structures merely as constraints on, rather than as causes of, individual choice and action. Once the effect of structures is duly noted, the economic model of rational behavior is quite adequate for the purposes of this book. Since I am here not primarily concerned with the formation of beliefs and preferences, the economic model coupled with the analysis of structural constraints is sufficient.

For the purposes of this book, therefore, given a set of structural constraints, a rational-choice explanation of an actor's behavior consists in showing this behavior to maximize his expected utility within those constraints. As we have seen, this means that, given a set of beliefs, and a set of available alternatives, the behavior in question is the best means to realize the actor's desires; that the reasons (beliefs and preferences) are the causes of the actor's behavior; that these reasons are free from contradiction (internally consistent); that the actor's preferences are transitive; and that, when probabilities are involved, the actor's calculations conform to the rules of probability calculus.

Strategic Rationality and Game Theory

Choice situations vary along two basic dimensions. The first has to do with the quality of information about the outcomes that result from alternative courses of action. According to this dimension, choice situations can be ones of certainty, risk, or uncertainty. A choice situation is one of certainty when the outcomes of each course of action can be predicted with certainty. Risk and uncertainty refer to situations in which an actor cannot uniquely predict the outcomes of his actions. In the case of risk, the actor can assign probabilities to the possible outcomes of a course of action; when such assignment is impossible, the situation is one of uncertainty.

The second dimension along which choice situations can be classified refers to the nature of the external constraints faced by the decision-maker. Depending on these, a situation can be *parametric* or *strategic*.[23] In a parametric situation the external constraints are constant with respect to the different courses of action the decision-maker may take. The rational decision-maker first assesses the state of the world, which then remains fixed as he evaluates which course of action will best realize his goals. Given a certain probability that it will rain, I can then decide whether the burden of carrying my umbrella is offset by the pleasure of staying dry.

The strategic situation is radically different. In a strategic situation, a decision-maker faces a world populated by other actors who condition their choices on what he and all other actors are likely to do. Before he chooses a course of action he must therefore anticipate what others are likely to do. And he must assume that all others will do the same. In other words, strategic situations are ones in which there is an interdependence of decisions. Each actor conditions his choices on the choices of others and assumes that all others will do the same.

Strategic choice situations, in which every actor is trying to guess what every other actor will do, might seem to lead to an infinite regress. But this is not the case. Assuming all actors are rational, the infinite regress can be circumvented by the notion of an equilibrium point.[24] This point is defined as the set of decisions (one for each actor) from which no actor has an incentive to deviate: no actor can improve his situation by deviating from his equilibrium decision as long as all other actors stick to theirs.

The theory that deals with strategic choice situations is game theory.[25] The part of game theory of interest here is noncooperative game theory. Whereas in cooperative games people can coordinate their choices to produce the best collective outcome, noncooperative games forbid this possibility. A game is defined as noncooperative if communication is impossible, or if players can communicate but agreements are not binding on them.

Noncooperative games are of two basic kinds. They are either constant-sum (zero-sum) or variable-sum (non-zero-sum) games. In a constant-sum game there is a fixed total amount of value to be divided by the actors, which means that one actor's gain necessarily entails losses for others. Such games are ones of pure conflict. In contrast, variable-sum games are characterized by a variable total amount to be divided by the players: the total amount will depend on the strategies chosen by the actors. Variable-sum games are therefore games in which there is a conflict of interests yet the actors also have an incentive to cooperate (in order to maximize the total sum of benefits). These mixed games of cooperation and conflict are particularly useful to the understanding of politics, since they best capture most concrete political situations.

The game I shall use in this book—the prisoner's dilemma—is a noncooperative, non-zero-sum game; it is therefore a mixed game of cooperation and conflict.[26] Its particular importance, however, resides in the fact that its structure prevents the players from getting their most preferred outcomes. In the prisoner's dilemma, rational action on the part of each individual brings about a state of affairs that is not the one preferred by any of the players: individual rationality brings about collective irrationality. As we shall see, this is precisely what happens in the case of democratic breakdowns.

The Prisoner's Dilemma

The general structure of the prisoner's dilemma can best be explained through the example of the game that gave it its name. Two persons, accomplices in a crime, are arrested and locked in different cells by the district attorney. Seeking to extract a confession, the district attorney takes advantage of the fact that the prisoners cannot communicate by proposing the following deal to each of them separately. He promises that, even if neither of them confesses, they will still get a ten-year sentence on other lesser offenses. If only one of them confesses, however, he promises him parole in seven years, while he threatens the less cooperative felon with a twenty-year sentence. Should both of them confess, they will each get fifteen years. This game is depicted in figure 2.

As shown in figure 2, each player has two possible strategies: don't confess (s_1) or confess (s_2). The rows of the matrix are reserved for the strategies of player 1, while the columns are for those of player 2. The payoffs for each possible outcome of the game appear in the four cells of the matrix. The first number is

Figure 2 The Two-Person Prisoner's Dilemma: An Example

		Prisoner 2	
		S1 Don't Confess	S2 Confess
Prisoner 1	S1	-10, -10	-20, -7
	S2	-7, -20	-15, -15

the payoff of player 1 and the second that of player 2. In the game depicted in figure 2, if both prisoners confess, for instance, both players will receive the same fifteen-year sentence.

In this case the payoffs are negative, of course, and the rational player will choose the strategy that minimizes his sentence. It can readily be shown that, for both players, the rational strategy is to confess. To see this, consider prisoner 1's choices. Suppose he thinks prisoner 2 will not confess. If that is the case, then 1 can either not confess and get ten years or confess and get only seven. So he should confess if he thinks 2 will not. Suppose now that 1 thinks 2 will confess. In this case, 1 can either not confess and get twenty years or confess and get fifteen. So in this case too 1 should confess. Thus no matter what the other prisoner does, 1 should confess.

The same logic applies to prisoner 2: no matter what 1 does, 2 is better off confessing. This means that both prisoners will confess and get fifteen years each. In sum, regardless of what the other prisoner does, and of what each prisoner thinks the other will do, if the prisoners are rational they will confess. Prisoner 1 will choose s_2 because it yields higher payoffs (−7, −15) than s_1 (−10, −20) whether prisoner 2 chooses to confess or not. The same is true of prisoner 2: he should choose s_2 because it yields higher payoffs than s_1 whatever prisoner 1 chooses to do. In other words, s_2 is the *dominant strategy* for both players, and the joint choice (s_2, s_2) is the equilibrium—or the solution—of the game because no actor can improve his situation by unilaterally choosing a different strategy.

Of course, it would be better for each player if *both* did not confess—they would then each get ten years rather than fifteen. However, because they cannot communicate, they cannot coordinate their choices, which means neither of them can be sure the other will not confess. But even if they could communicate, and agreed not to confess, it would be dangerous for either of the prisoners to honor the agreement. Since there is no way of enforcing the agreement, each prisoner has a strong incentive to violate the agreement, for in doing so, he might reduce his sentence by three years. Herein lies the peculiarity of the prisoner's dilemma. The game is such that there is an outcome both players would jointly and unanimously prefer to the one they actually choose, yet the structure of incentives prevents them from achieving that outcome. It is a game in which "individual rationality leads to a worse outcome for both players than is possible."[27]

The general structure of the two-person prisoner's dilemma is depicted in figure 3. Each player has two strategies: either cooperate or defect. Cooperation need not be a good thing; players may cooperate in a murder. In the example above, cooperation meant *not* confessing to a crime. Player 1 chooses a row, either cooperating or defecting. Player 2 *simultaneously* chooses a column (neither player knows what the other is going to do). Their choices result in one of the four possible outcomes represented by the four cells of the table in figure 3.

If both players cooperate, they receive *R*, the *reward* for mutual cooperation. If one player cooperates and the other defects, the cooperating player gets *S*, the *sucker's* payoff, while the defecting player gets *T*, the *temptation* to defect. In the example above, the prisoner who does not confess gets twenty years—the sucker's payoff—while the one who does gets only seven—the temptation to defect. Finally, if both players defect, they get *P*, the *punishment* for mutual defection.

The order of the payoffs of the four outcomes defines the game. As our example shows, the best a player can do is get *T*, the temptation to defect when the other player cooperates. The next best payoff is *R*, the reward for mutual cooperation. In third place comes *P*, the punishment for mutual defection. Finally, the worst a player can get is *S*, the sucker's payoff. Therefore each

Figure 3 The Two-Person Prisoner's Dilemma: The General Game

		Player 2	
		Cooperate	Defect
Player 1	Cooperate	R, R	S, T
	Defect	T, S	P, P

player's preference ranking from best to worst is *T*, *R*, *P*, and *S* ($T > R > P > S$). As we saw in the example above, given this preference ordering, both players will defect and get *P*, which is their third preference. Because the players cannot make any binding agreements, they can always get the sucker's payoff. To avoid this, they have to defect in spite of the fact that they do worse than if both had cooperated. The prisoner's dilemma game is thus a highly abstract representation of situations in which the "pursuit of self-interest by each leads to a poor outcome for all."[28]

The Repeated Prisoner's Dilemma

As shown above, when the prisoner's dilemma is played only once, cooperation is impossible. When it is played repeatedly, however, cooperation is a possible outcome of the game. In the next chapter, I am going to argue that the one-shot game is the most appropriate to model the political conflict leading to the breakdown of democracy. Since questions might arise as to whether the repeated game might not be an adequate representation of that conflict, I will discuss here the basic features of the repeated prisoner's dilemma and explain in the following chapter why it does not apply to the situations studied in this book.

That the repeated prisoner's dilemma can generate cooperation has been known by experimental game-theorists since the fifties and was theoretically proven only in the seventies.[29] Repeated play can generate cooperation because it allows for correlated strategies. In other words, repetitions allow players to "choose their strategy contingent upon their opponent's choice in the previous round(s)."[30] A player can warn his opponent, for example, that he will cooperate in the first round and will continue to do so as long as his opponent cooperates. If the latter defects even once, he will defect in all other rounds of the game. If the opponent believes this threat, he should cooperate, because mutual cooperation improves the players' payoffs: they will both receive *R* instead of *P* in each interaction.

The problem with this argument, however, is that (assuming complete information) it holds only for games with an infinite number of repetitions.[31] And human beings do not usually play infinite games. When the game is played only a known finite number of times, the players will not cooperate. The reason for this is given by the "backwards induction" argument. Because the last round is known in advance, each player anticipates a defection by the other player in that last known round, since there will then be no future to influence. Knowing this, both players will also defect in the penultimate round, and so on, all the way back to the first round, when both players will defect because there is no future to influence. Thus, when the prisoner's dilemma is played a known finite number of times, both players will defect in each and every round of the game.

In an attempt to show how a finite repeated prisoner's dilemma can generate cooperation, Robert Axelrod has argued that if the number of repetitions is unknown, a finite repeated game can lead to cooperation. After acknowledging the impossibility of cooperation when the number of repetitions is known, Axelrod goes on to say that "with an indefinite number of interactions, cooperation can emerge."[32] Unfortunately, as Tsebelis and others have shown, although Axelrod's conjecture is still widely believed to be true, it is false.[33]

There is no reason to believe that finite indefinite games would generate different results from other finite games where the number of repetitions is known. Even when the number of repetitions is unknown, if the game is finite, it can be shown that the appropriate strategy is ALLD ("all defect," or both players defect in each round of the game). As Tsebelis puts it:

> Consider playing a prisoners' dilemma game either twice or three times, but not knowing which will be the case. You can reason as follows: if I play twice, the optimal strategy is ALLD; if I play three iterations, then the optimal strategy is still ALLD; therefore no matter what the actual number of iterations turns out to be, I should still use ALLD. More generally, if both players know they are going to interact a finite number of times, there is some finite number that they both know will never be reached (say 100^{100}). If they play a one-shot game, they would both defect. In the event the game is played twice, they would both adopt ALLD (as the backwards induction argument suggests); the same strategy is adopted if the number of iterations is three or four, and so on. In fact, one can develop an inductive argument that

> for any finite number of rounds, ALLD is the best response of both players to each other. Therefore, no matter what the exact number of iterations turns out to be, each player will still play ALLD.[34]

Thus, whether the number of rounds is known or not, if the game is finite, mutual cooperation is impossible. Backwards induction eliminates the possibility of cooperation in finite games even when the number of iterations is unknown. Just like in the finite game where the number of repetitions is known, backwards induction precludes cooperation when the game is indefinite by eliminating the possibility of contingent, or correlated, strategies. If backwards induction tells you that your opponent will play ALLD no matter what you do, you should also play ALLD lest you collect the sucker's payoff. Furthermore, this conclusion holds not only when one is playing against a rational opponent who uses backwards induction. Even if one's opponent is kind and is willing to cooperate at every turn of the game, the rational response is to play ALLD, since this strategy would then give one the best payoff, *T*, in each round of the game. In a word, then, in finite games, whether definite or indefinite, "all defect" is always the optimal strategy.

If the indefiniteness of the repeated game cannot explain why the players in Axelrod's experiments chose cooperative strategies, what does explain this? Why did many of the sophisticated players in Axelrod's tournaments ignore the prescriptions of backwards induction and choose strategies that never prescribed defection first? The answer to these questions was recently given by Fudenberg and Maskin, who prove the "folk theorem" about repeated games.[35] These two game-theorists proved that—provided the players valued the future sufficiently (little discounting)—not only infinite games but also finite ones can generate mutual cooperation. Finite games (provided the number of repetitions is sufficiently large) can do so, however, only if there is incomplete information. Only when a player is uncertain about his opponent's payoffs will cooperation be rational for him. Consider a player who does not know his opponent's payoffs. If he believes there is a chance his opponent's payoffs are such that mutual cooperation is rational for him, he may choose to cooperate and mutual cooperation may then be the outcome of each round of the game. It is therefore not the indefiniteness of a finite game, as Axelrod would have it, that makes cooperation possible. It is, rather, incomplete information, and a sufficiently large number of repetitions, that allows mutual cooperation to emerge.

That cooperation *can* emerge from a finite repeated prisoner's dilemma with incomplete information does not mean, of course, that it will. Mutual cooperation is only one possible outcome among many. This makes it very difficult to make any predictions about such repeated games.[36] Nevertheless, one can make predictions about the likelihood that a finite repeated game with incomplete information will generate mutual cooperation. As Tsebelis has shown, one of the implications of Fudenberg and Maskin's proof is that "when the rewards for cooperation increase or the rewards for defection decrease, cooperation becomes more likely (cooperation requires shorter time horizons to develop)."[37] To conclude, then, cooperation is *possible* in finite repeated prisoner's dilemma games only if the players believe that the chance there will be a relatively large number of repetitions is high, if they care enough about future payoffs (little discounting), and if they are uncertain about each other's payoffs. And cooperation is *likely* if the payoffs for cooperation are sufficiently high relative to the payoffs for defection.

5 THE PRISONER'S DILEMMA AND THE COLLAPSE OF DEMOCRACY

As I have already argued, the structural perspective on the breakdown of democracy would have us believe it was inevitable.[1] According to this point of view, the severe structural problems Latin American economies began to face in the sixties were such that, if capitalist growth were to resume, the growing demands for reforms and redistribution had to be contained.

This could not be done, structuralists argue, within the context of a democratic regime. Coupled with the abundant growth of early industrialization, democratic institutions had facilitated the mobilization and organization of both urban and rural workers, as well as the flourishing of a variety of leftist organizations, all of which formed a powerful movement for social, economic, and political change. In this democratic atmosphere, the pressure for redistribution and reform could only grow. By the early sixties, reform had become the focus of public debate in much of Latin America. The lower classes and the left were pushing for redistributive policies and sweeping reforms, ranging from changes in wage and tax policy to a restructuring of the educational system and a major redistribution of land. Clearly, then, only a suspension of democratic rights could have arrested this flood of demands for socioeconomic and political change.

According to the structuralist point of view, as long as the economy continued to grow, severe class conflict could be averted. The demands of the increasingly powerful urban and rural workers were only mildly disruptive during the early phase of industrialization because they could be accommodated by the relatively high rates of economic growth that characterized that stage. But this was only a passing phase, after which Latin American economies were bound to stagnate. The structural limits of dependent capitalist development were such that stagnation would follow the exuberance of the initial spurt of industrialization. When, in the sixties, the allegedly structurally induced stagnation came, there was no longer any room to meet the redistributive demands of the lower classes. The structural problems inherent in the process of dependent capitalist development had created a rift between economic growth, on the one hand, and democracy and reforms, on the other.

The Possibility of Reform

The structural explanation of the breakdown of democracy would thus lead us to conclude that the structure of mature dependent capitalism is incompatible with social reform and democracy. To continue growing, mature dependent capitalism must repress the demands of the working classes and the left. Since workers are usually unwilling to relinquish the benefits acquired during the early stages of industrialization, as dependent capitalism matures it perforce exacerbates class conflict. According to structuralists, this is what happened in the sixties and seventies in Latin America. The working class had no alternative but to go to war against the dominant classes, and these, in turn, had to call in the military to repress workers and establish an authoritarian regime. For the structuralists there was really no room for compromise, no room even for gradual, moderate reform within a democratic context.

The structural explanation is not all wrong. The economic crisis of the sixties did in fact generate much tension between capitalist structures and democratic institutions. And it was definitely unfavorable to redistribution and reform. As we saw, however, structuralists have overstated their case. Theirs is a theory which Albert Hirschman has repeatedly criticized for being an "either major structural change or doom" theory, that is, for turning what are mere *difficulties* concerning economic growth into *structural impossibilities*.[2] The evidence collected in previous chapters of this book confirms Hirschman's views.[3] There was much more room for economic expansion within a capitalist *and* democratic framework than the structural theorists suspected. There is little reason to believe that authoritarian regimes were necessary to pull Latin American countries out of the economic crisis they experienced in the sixties.

In the next two chapters I will offer much evidence showing that, in spite of all the tumult of the sixties, there also was considerable room for passing moderate reforms within the boundaries of democratic institutions. I do not mean to imply that there were no limits to the depth and scope of change Latin American capitalism could bear. Radical reforms were, of course, out of the question. But there were many significant proposals for reform that were perfectly compatible with capitalist institutions. I see no reason to presume that many of the reforms proposed by the Brazilian left, for instance, could not have been enacted within the context of a dependent capitalist democracy.[4] Enfranchising illiterates, granting political rights to enlisted military men, or restructuring the educational system were certainly threatening to many. But these were by no means precluded by the structural requirements of capitalist accumulation and reproduction.

Even agrarian reform, perhaps the most threatening of all proposed reforms, could have been implemented in its more moderate version. The Frei administration, for example, successfully enacted and began to implement a substantial program of agrarian reform in the sixties.[5] And, during most of Goulart's brief government in Brazil, the prospects for a moderate program of land redistribution were extremely good. In a recent work on the causes of the Brazilian coup of 1964, Argelina Figueiredo shows that the majority of the population as well as of the politicians in Congress was in principle favorable to a moderate program of agrarian reform.[6] This is true not only for the left and the center of the political spectrum. Among right-leaning politicians there was also much support for moderate reform. It was only a minority of extremists that rejected any kind of reform.

Much of what we know, then, goes against the grain of the structuralist thesis. There was sufficient room for compromise and conciliation during the crisis of the sixties, which means that the popular classes and the left, as well as the dominant classes, had choices other than radicalizing and engaging in mortal combat. However, if it is true that a majority among both left and right could have compromised around a moderate program of reforms, why is it that they ended up radicalizing and provoking the breakdown few people really wanted?

The answer is that the groups that could have compromised—the moderate left and the moderate right—were caught in a situation best explained by a prisoner's dilemma game. *Given the structure of their preferences,* the two moderate camps were caught in a political situation in which the rational pursuit of their own interest would lead to an outcome they both wanted to avoid—no reforms, no democracy—an outcome that was clearly worse than the possible cooperative one which included moderate reforms under a democratic regime.

To show that this was the case, I will now analyze the relationship between the two moderate camps and the relationships between each of these and their counterparts at the extremes of the political spectrum. The analysis that follows is an abstract representation of the political conflict leading to the demise of democracy in Latin America. The actors involved in the conflict are here defined abstractly, without much reference to particulars. My purpose in the present chapter is to draw out as sharply as possible the causal mechanism driving the actors toward the collapse of democratic institutions. I have therefore purposefully omitted distracting references to concrete situations until the next two chapters, where I will flesh out in full detail the model developed here.

The Moderates' Dilemma

The Moderates' Preferences

In the situation analyzed here, a progressive president wishes to implement a program of major socioeconomic and political reforms. But he cannot do so unless Congress passes the needed legislation. Given the highly controversial nature of the issues involved in enacting those reforms, the political situation is potentially explosive. The situation is such that, to a large extent, the very preservation of democratic institutions is contingent upon the passage by Congress of legislation enabling the social and political changes desired by the government and by the majority of the population.

In Congress, there are four basic groups: the extreme left, the moderate left, the moderate right, and the extreme right. These groups operate within a multiparty system, with parties ranging from the far left to the far right. Each group does not necessarily belong to a single party; it may be spread over several. Although the two extremist groups are clearly separated along party lines, the moderates need not be so. Any single centrist party may have different mixes of the two types of moderates. Regardless of the specific distribution of groups across parties, however, the key to an understanding of the breakdown of democracy lies in the strategic interaction of the four groups involved.

Although the multiparty systems typical of the situations analyzed in this book are of the kind Sartori has shown to be prone to polarization, there is no reason to suppose, as I have shown in chapter 3, either that they will automatically radicalize or that such a radicalization will necessarily lead to a breakdown of democratic institutions.[7] Although these multiparty systems are characterized by antisystem parties, bilateral oppositions, ideological patterning, an occupied center, irresponsible oppositions, political outbidding, polarization, and centrifugal drives, the activation of those drives and the consequent radicalization and breakdown of the system are contingent upon the strategic interaction among moderates and extremists of the left and the right. Multiparty systems with centrifugal drives, as Sartori himself acknowledged, can function indefinitely without radicalization. This is precisely why structural explanations that see the causes of breakdown in political structures and institutions fail to explain the collapse of democratic regimes. The explanation of such a collapse must be sought elsewhere. It must be sought in the strategic interaction involving the four groups of moderates and extremists, to the analysis of which I shall now turn.

In the model I propose, although moderates share a wish to implement reform gradually and within the parameters of the democratic regime, they are divided by their politico-ideological preferences. The moderate left holds egalitarian goals in common with the extreme left, but wants to achieve them gradually and democratically, without resorting to violence. On the other hand, the moderate right is just as leery of reforms as the extreme right, especially those involving changes in capitalist institutions or in the provisions of the Constitution. Unlike the extremists, however, the moderates at the right are willing to make substantial concessions to the left when these are absolutely necessary to defuse conflict and preserve liberal-democratic institutions. Right-leaning moderates are far more pragmatic than their counterparts at the extreme. Nevertheless, they drive a hard bargain with the moderate left; they seldom concede an inch beyond what is necessary.

Thus, though both moderate sides are willing to enact reforms, they are likely to differ significantly on the scope and depth of those reforms. Both sides may be willing to expropriate and redistribute unproductive land, for example, but disagree on the amount and type of land that should be expropriated or on the form of compensation to the owners of the expropriated land. In Brazil, for instance, though moderates agreed on the need for a substantial land reform, they disagreed on issues involving the criteria of expropriation and the form and amount of compensation for expropriated land.[8]

Given that the two moderate camps agree on the basic need for reform, their disagreements on the scope and depth of the reforms are far from irreconcilable. Moreover, there are strong pressures and powerful incentives working in favor of cooperation. In the first place, the moderates know that a failure to pass reforms through the normal constitutional channels will almost certainly lead to a radicalization of the political system. Moderate congressmen of both the left and the right are aware that a failure to pass reform legislation is likely to lead to violent protest on the part of the extreme left, which, in turn, would lead to retaliation on the part of the extreme right. After a few rounds of radical action, the moderates would have no option but to close ranks with the extremists. No matter which side ultimately won, this radicalization would entail a breakdown of democratic institutions.

Saving the democratic regime is not the only incentive to reach an agreement on reforms. Should the moderates pass a program of reforms that is acceptable to the majority of the population, they would no doubt benefit a great deal from an electoral point of view. By cooperating with each other, they would not only strengthen the foundations of the democratic regime and thus enhance its stability, but also isolate the extremists at the opposite ends of the ideological spectrum. These would lose much of their justification for existing, which is based, at the left, on a lack of responsiveness to the demands from the lower classes, and at the right, on the fear of radical change.

Finally, in the situations of interest to this book, the two moderate sides not only have major incentives to reach an agreement but also the means to pass the legislation necessary to effect social, economic, and political change. The two moderate sides are roughly matched in Congress. Neither side can pass the needed legislation alone, but together they command the amount of votes necessary to enact major reforms. In some cases, a simple majority vote is needed. But when a constitutional amendment is involved, two-thirds of the vote is required. Whichever the case, together the two moderate camps control in Congress the necessary numbers to pass the legislation required.[9]

The Moderates' Fears

If each moderate side stands to gain a great deal from enacting reforms, and together they have the means to do so, one would expect them actually to reach an agreement and to pass the necessary legislation. Yet such a prediction would be clearly mistaken because it does not take into account the fears moderates have of each other. These fears stem partly from their preferences and opportunities, and partly from each side's relationship with the extremists in its own camp.

The moderate right fears that the moderate left might use any concession on reforms as a first step toward imposing ever more radical changes. Given that the moderate left's ultimate goal is to enact a program of all-encompassing reforms, there is nothing to guarantee that it will stop at the more modest program temporarily negotiated with the right. The moderate left could join forces with the radicals in pushing ever broader and more comprehensive social reforms. Every concession from the moderate right could be turned into a victory, increasing at each turn the popular power of the left. In this fashion, the movement for reforms could swell and gain momentum, making it almost impossible for the right and the military to prevent a radical transformation of the country. Even worse, the moderate leftists' commitment to democracy could flag, and they might be tempted to join the radicals in staging a leftist takeover.

The fear of this possibility is based on the fact that the moderate left has strong ties to the radicals, and allows the latter to increase its power and influence in the political system. In the political situations analyzed here, the moderate left controls the lion's share of governmental resources—since the chief executive is a progressive leader of the moderate left—which it partly uses to strengthen the hand of its radical allies. In exchange for these favors, the radicals can mobilize popular support for the moderates, either in the form of votes or in the form of strikes and demonstrations. Although the extremists of the left may be a minority in Congress, they are a significant force outside the legislature. They can count on popular leaders, important positions in the government's labor bureaucracy, and a wide network of labor organizations to mobilize popular support for their own or their allies' objectives.

That the moderates exchange favors with the radicals does not necessarily mean that they harbor secret revolutionary intentions. Moderate politicians of the left may be using the radicals only to increase their power within the democratic system, believing that the radicals present no real threat to the regime. Though this may be the case, the fact that the moderate left allows the radicals to flourish is bound to breed a great deal of nervousness among the ranks of the moderate right. Uncertain about the strength of the moderate left's commitment to democratic procedures, the moderates of the right will suspect that moderate leftists are playing a dangerous double game. After all, these could be willing to compromise and negotiate in the shorter run, while setting the stage to impose a far more radical set of reforms in the longer run. Even worse, the moderate leftists could be tempted, as explained above, to shed their initial commitment to democracy and to join the radicals in staging a leftist takeover.

On the other hand, the moderate leftists also have deep-seated fears concerning the moderate right. The moderate left fears that the moderates of the right might be actually unwilling to make more than token concessions toward implementing reforms. They suspect that, should they exert any pressure to compel the moderate right to pass more progressive legislation, the moderate right will lend their support to the extremists of the right to help them bring about a reactionary military regime. In this way, the moderate right could preempt the left's unique historical opportunity to usher in the social changes they so highly value.

The suspicions of the moderate left stem from the fact that

politicians of the moderate right maintain close connections with extreme right-wingers. These connections serve two different purposes. In the first place, the moderates form electoral alliances with extremists of the right; they may also form coalitions with the extremists to pass or block legislation in Congress. Secondly, the moderate politicians of the right maintain relations with the extremists for defensive purposes. Given their fears of the left, they want to be in contact with the extremists in case there is need for quick action to stop the left from taking over.

Though the moderates of the right are far from sharing the objectives of the extreme right—and maintain purely instrumental and defensive relations with the extremists—their ties to the extreme right-wingers will undoubtedly trigger the suspicions of the moderate leftists, who are bound to believe that the moderate rightists are also playing a double game. After all, these could be negotiating only to bide their time, until they find the pretext that would allow them and the extremists to incite the military to intervene.

Needless to say, the relations between each moderate side and its extremist counterpart breed a great deal of fear on both sides, which, to say the least, is not conducive to reaching an agreement on legislation to implement a program of reforms. Even though both moderate sides may genuinely prefer a democratic settlement on reforms, the moderate right will be afraid to make substantial concessions to the leftists, lest these take advantage of the situation to eventually push through ever more radical reforms—or worse; and the moderate left will be afraid to make major concessions to the rightists, lest these rob it of its unique historical opportunity to reform the country.

The moderates, however, will make an effort to assuage each other's fears. At least in the medium run, both moderate sides genuinely prefer to reach a peaceful agreement and stand to gain a great deal from it. To this end, moderate leaders will attempt to reassure each other by reasserting their willingness to compromise, and by trying to persuade the extremists to refrain from radicalizing the situation. But these attempts are not likely to work.

Each one of the moderate sides cannot effectively control its extremists because, in addition to all their other uses, the extremists also serve to put pressure on the other moderates. The radical leftists help the moderate left to extract concessions from the moderate right, while the extremists on the right help the moderate rightists contain the demands of the moderate left. The problem, of course, is that, in doing so, the radicals also stimulate the mutual fears of the moderates. As the radicals get out of hand, the moderates are thus forced to turn around and attempt to placate them. Since they profit from their alliance with the radicals, however, the moderates have little to threaten them with; they can only placate the radicals by making further concessions to them. Such concessions, of course, will only reinforce the suspicions of each moderate side that the other side is playing a double game in collusion with the extremists.

Moreover, the extremists may not want to cooperate. On the contrary, they have more to gain by playing on the hesitation and mutual fears of the moderates to turn the situation to their advantage.

The Extremists' Strategy

Unlike the moderates, the minorities at the opposite extremes of the political spectrum are unwilling to compromise over a program of reforms. They are perfectly willing to sacrifice democratic institutions to other ends. The extremists of the right are not against liberal democracy, as long as it does not nurture demands for social reform. Right-wingers, however, are quick to ask for military intervention when the threat of reforms looms large.

As for leftist radicals, they are of course openly hostile to liberal democratic institutions. They are willing, however, to work in a democratic framework, but only momentarily, until they have enough power to transform it from within. Leftist radicals see in the political situation a unique historical opportunity to seize power and effect a radical transformation of the country.

Neither group of extremists wants the moderates to reach an agreement to pass a piecemeal program of reforms. On the contrary, both want to split the moderates and drive them into a more radical course of action. The extremists of the right want the moderates of the right to join them in blocking reforms in Congress, or in persuading the military to oust the progressive government. Without the support of the moderates, extreme right-wingers cannot hope to do so, for the military are unlikely to intervene if the majority of moderates opposes a coup.[10] As to the extremists of the left, they want the moderate leftists to join them in forcing Congress to pass radical reforms, or, short of this, to impose these radical changes by extraconstitutional means. Without the support of the moderates, the radicals cannot hope to mobilize sufficient popular support, nor the necessary resources, to achieve their radical objectives.

To split the moderates and drive them to take a more radical course of action, the extremists must play on the moderates' fears. Each moderate side's worst nightmare is that, in cooperating with the other side, it will lose everything. It could not only suffer betrayal from the other side, which is tempted to take advantage of its cooperation, but also lose the support of the radicals—and possibly of other followers—within its own camp. Knowing this, the extremists' strategy is to play on both the fear moderates have of each other and the fear they have of losing support from their own allies.

To play on these fears, extremists use the following tactics. Whenever the moderates show any willingness to cooperate with each other, each extremist side will stage as visible and disruptive a campaign as possible, denouncing the moderates on its own side for caving in to the demands of the other side. Afraid of losing support from its own constituency, and unable to cut its ties to the radicals, each moderate side will then try to accommodate its own radical allies. But this will inevitably reinforce the suspicions of the moderates on the other side. Consequently, both moderate sides will no longer be as ready to cooperate as they initially were. Thus, by attacking the moderates in their own camp whenever they show any willingness to reach an agreement with the other side, the radicals reinforce all the fears of both moderate sides, splitting them apart and preventing them from cooperating toward reaching an agreement on reforms.

To put it more concretely, whenever the moderates show any sign of making concessions to each other, the extremists of the left and the right will attack them. The radical leftists will attack the moderate leftists, accusing them of caving in to the "reactionary" demands of the right, while the extremist right-wingers will attack the moderate rightists, accusing them of caving in to the "subversive" demands of the radicals. This will force the moderates to back away from their initial concessions, in an attempt to accommodate the extremists. In doing so, however, each moderate side will be reinforcing the other's suspicion that it is in fact colluding with its radical allies.

Playing on these growing mutual suspicions, the extremists can then feed off each other's radical activities to set in motion a spiral of radicalization. Every time one group of extremists resorts to radical action and the moderates on the same side try to accommodate them, the other group of extremists can seize this opportunity not only to accuse those moderates of colluding with the extremists but also to justify a "defensive" radicalization on its own part. It can thus set in motion another round of radicalization, which in turn creates the opportunity for yet another one, and so on, driving the two moderate sides further and further apart.

In this way, the instrumental uses the moderates make of the extremists afford the latter an opportunity to set in motion a spiral of radicalization which undermines all efforts to implement reforms through normal democratic channels. In forming alliances with the extremists, the moderates can thus end up promoting the objectives of the extremists at the expense of their own.

The Moderates' Dilemma

To prevent radicalization, and to restore the mutual confidence necessary to negotiate an agreement democratically, the moderates have but one option open to them. Since they cannot tame their radical allies, the two moderate sides can reassure each other only by cutting their ties to the extremists. To reassure the moderate right that it will stop somewhere in the middle of the road between token reforms and radical change, that it will follow a social-democratic rather than a socialist or communist program, the moderate left has to condemn unequivocally the radical objectives and tactics of the extreme left. Similarly, to reassure the moderate left, the moderate right must unambiguously repudiate the extreme right and condemn any future intervention by the military. In a word, the moderates must publicly commit themselves to uphold democratic procedures, firmly break with the extremists, and vow to take action against them if they persist in a radical course of action. Unfortunately, neither moderate side can unilaterally break with its extremist counterpart. And no agreement between them to do so simultaneously can be binding.

To see that neither side can unilaterally break with its extremist ally, consider what would happen if the moderate right severed its ties to the extremists while the moderate left did not. In repudiating the extremists of the right, and publicly condemning any attempt at military intervention, the moderates of the right would make it extremely difficult for any such intervention to occur. Short of a wide base of support among the moderates of the right, the military would be unlikely to intervene in politics.[11] Thus, by forcefully condemning the activities of extreme right-wingers, the moderates of the right would certainly reassure the moderates of the left, and restore the confidence necessary to reaching a peaceful agreement on reforms. But, without the threat posed by a united right and a potential military coup, the moderates of the right would lose much of their capacity to contain the demands of the left. The moderate leftists and their radical allies would thus be in a much stronger position to push through their radical program of reforms.

It is true that, should the left take excessive advantage of the right's breaking with the extremists, the moderate right could always turn around and try to reconstruct its alliance with the extreme right-wingers and the conservative military. By then, however, it might be too late. The left might have grown too powerful to be stopped, or the right too divided to stage a successful military intervention. And, even if a military intervention could still succeed, its risks and costs would be much higher. The contemplation of such possibilities, then, would be sufficient to deter the moderate right from unilaterally breaking with its extremist allies.

By the same token, the moderate left cannot unilaterally break with the extremists in its own camp. Suppose the moderate leftists broke with the radicals, and threatened to take action against them if they persisted in radicalizing the situation, while the moderate right did not break its relations with extremist right-wingers. If the radicals persisted, which they almost certainly would, the moderates of the left would be forced to join the right in taking repressive measures against them. This would obviously reassure the moderate right, but would also leave the moderate left at its mercy. With the threat of radicalization and mass insurrection out of the way, the moderate right and its extremist allies would have much less incentive to heed the demands of the moderate left.

We can now fully understand the situation constraining the moderates. The situation is such that the rewards for passing a moderate program of reforms are high for each of the moderate sides. They both want to enact reforms without disrupting the democratic process. But a successful negotiation of a program of reforms is contingent on each moderate side making an unequivocal break with its extremist counterpart. Since both sides stand to gain from a successful negotiation, one would think that they would both break with their extremist partners.

Each of the moderate camps knows, however, that its opponent would benefit even more if it broke with its extremists and its opponent did not. The moderate left knows that, if it were the one to break with the extremists in its camp while the moderate right were to avoid such a break, it would be incapable of extracting concessions from the right. In this case, the moderate right would have a complete victory: it would make a minimum of concessions toward reform and maintain the status quo. On the other hand, if the moderate right were to break with its extremists and the moderate left did not, it would be incapable of restraining the left. The moderate left then would carry the day: in one way or another, it would push through an all-encompassing program of reforms.

Given this structure of incentives, each one of the moderate sides will not break with its extremist counterpart unless it can be assured that the other one also will. But nothing can give them this assurance. For no agreement is binding in this situation; each side has a strong incentive to renege on a promise to break with its extremist counterpart. Since neither of the moderate sides will break with the extremists, no agreement on reforms is possible. As a consequence the extreme left is likely to radicalize even further, threatening popular insurrection, which, in turn, would frighten the moderate right, causing it to close ranks with the extreme right. Depending on the resources of each group, the final outcome will be an autocratic regime of either the left or the right.

As the reader may have already noticed, the relations between the two moderate camps can be depicted as a prisoner's dilemma—in the present case, a moderates' dilemma game. The way the moderates' dilemma works is shown in figure 4.

In this game played by the two moderate sides, to cooperate

Figure 4 The Moderates' Dilemma

		Moderate Right	
		Breaks (Cooperate)	Doesn't Break (Defect)
Moderate Left	Breaks (Cooperate)	R, R Agreement on Reforms Democracy Preserved	S, T Left Defeated Minimal Reforms
	Doesn't Break (Defect)	T, S Right Defeated Radical Reforms	P, P Agreement Impossible Democracy Collapses

means breaking with one's extremist counterpart and to defect means not to break with that group. If both players break with their respective extremist camps, they both do fairly well. Their reward (*R*) for cooperation is that an agreement over moderate reforms is now possible and democracy can be preserved. Furthermore, each side becomes far less dependent on its extremist counterpart, while their political power relative to each other remains roughly the same. They now have a good chance of reaping additional political dividends from successfully passing a popular package of progressive legislation without damaging democratic institutions.

If the moderate left breaks with the extremists but the moderate right does not, it receives its worst payoff—the sucker's payoff (*S*)—because it becomes far more vulnerable to the right, loses much if not all of its bargaining power, and achieves almost nothing in terms of reform. On the other hand, the moderate right obtains its best payoff—the temptation to defect (*T*)—because it no longer needs to make major concessions to the left.

If the moderate right breaks with the extremists but the moderate left does not, it also receives its worst payoff—the sucker's payoff (*S*)—because it becomes more vulnerable to attack from the left, loses much if not all of its threatening power, and is therefore far less capable of arresting the movement toward sweeping reforms. On the other hand, the moderate left obtains its best payoff—the temptation to defect (*T*)—because it can impose on the right its all-encompassing program of reforms.

Finally, when both sides do not break with the extremes, they are both punished for mutual defection (*P*). Not even moderate reforms are now possible, the moderates join the radicals, and an all-out confrontation between the left and the right ensues.

Although both moderate sides prefer reaching an agreement (*R*) to a confrontation (*P*), they prefer a confrontation (*P*) to a complete defeat (*S*). This is so because both sides believe they have a good chance to prevail should a confrontation take place. Leftists think they have sufficient power to mobilize the masses to pressure Congress into passing radical reforms before the military can intervene, while the right believes it can persuade the military to stop the left from imposing these radical reforms.

For understandable reasons—which I will examine in the following chapter—in the Latin American case it is the left that usually overestimates its capacity to win a confrontation. The final outcome of the moderates' dilemma is therefore a military coup that establishes a dictatorship of the right.

From figure 4 and the discussion above, we can see that the order of the payoffs follows that of the prisoner's dilemma as depicted in figures 2 and 3. For each of the moderate camps, the best payoff is *T*, the temptation to defect, and the worst is *S*, the sucker's payoff. Since *R* is clearly better than *P*, we have the rank ordering of the prisoner's dilemma—$T > R > P > S$. Given that no agreements to cooperate (break alliance with its extremists) are binding (because, as I have already said, there is nothing to guarantee that a player will stick to a promise to cooperate), each moderate side will defect. As figure 4 shows, defection is the dominant strategy for each player: each player stands to gain more from defection no matter what the other player does. In other words, each side will not break with its extreme counterpart, no agreement on reforms will be made, an all-out confrontation will ensue, and the democratic regime will collapse.

Qualifying the Model

I have just presented the breakdown of democratic regimes as the outcome of a mixed game of cooperation and conflict—a one-shot prisoner's dilemma involving moderates and extremists of the left and the right. Before I go on to apply this model to explain the cases of Brazil and Chile, I want to say a few words of caution concerning the range of cases to which the above model applies, and to clarify my choice of a one-shot (as opposed to a repeated) prisoner's dilemma.

There is good reason to believe that the model I presented here is relevant to a range of cases wider than the two I analyze in this book. Brazil and Chile are classic instances of a broader class of cases of the breakdown of democracy. Just as in Brazil and Chile, in most contemporary Latin American cases of breakdown, and in some European cases before the Second World War, the collapse of democracy followed a process of radicalization of the left and the right that moderate forces were unable to prevent. Since my model states the conditions under which moderate forces cannot avert radicalization and breakdown, there is thus good reason to presume that it can also explain those other cases.

It is perhaps important to note, however, that my model does *not* imply that all conflicts among moderates and extremists will bring about a collapse of democratic institutions. If that were the case, there would be many more breakdowns than there actually are. My model only states that democratic regimes will collapse if the conflict among moderates and extremists is of the kind described by the prisoner's dilemma explained in this book. And many conflicts involving moderates and extremists are of a kind different from the ones described by the prisoner's dilemma. Many such conflicts, therefore, do not preclude mutual cooperation between the moderates.

In my model, both extremists have adopted a short-run radical strategy and the moderates are split in terms of their politico-ideological views and goals. But this need not be the case at all. One or both of the extremist groups may not radicalize. If the extremists believe they can win only in the longer run, they will seek smaller incremental victories in the shorter run. They will then join the moderates on their side in an effort to turn out the best piecemeal reforms possible at the time. In this case, the left and the right would be playing a cooperative game of bargaining rather than a prisoner's dilemma. This is the kind of bargaining game the communists of many Latin American countries played in the forties and fifties. Because communists then believed that a socialist society could not emerge before the "bourgeois revolution" ran its course, they opted for a strategy of cooperating with the "reformist bourgeoisie" toward the achievement of gradual change. The situation changed in the late fifties, when much of the left radicalized and the game played by moderates and extremists turned into a prisoner's dilemma.

Even when the extremists radicalize, however, the preferences and payoffs of the moderates may be such as to lead them to cooperate in checking the extremists and implementing a program of gradual reforms. If the great majority of moderates shares the same basic political views and goals, the extremists will be unable to radicalize the polity, and the united moderates will be able to cooperate and preserve democratic institutions. If this were the case, the game played by the moderates would not be a mixed game of cooperation and conflict like the prisoner's dilemma. It would be, rather, a cooperative game with some bargaining among moderates. A possible example of such a situation is that of Chile under Frei, where the moderates in the Christian Democratic Party were sufficiently united to check the extremists and implement a comprehensive set of socioeconomic reforms within the context of a democratic regime.

It is not my intention to chart here all the possibilities concerning the relations among moderates and extremists. All I am trying to argue is that the mere presence of the four groups of moderates and extremists does not necessarily entail a breakdown of the democratic regime. Such a breakdown will occur only if the preferences and payoffs of the moderates and extremists are such as to constitute a prisoner's dilemma. This game describes one type—that which leads to democratic breakdown—among other possible types of relations involving moderates and extremists of the left and the right. The prisoner's dilemma models the type of situation in which the extremists on both sides are unyielding and the moderates, although they share a preference for gradual reform, are split in both their political views and their organizational basis. There is thus some ground for mutual cooperation between the moderates, but, given that the extremists are uncompromising, the overwhelming punishment for unilateral cooperation precludes a cooperative outcome.

It is also the peculiar characteristics of this type of situation that make it a one-shot rather than a repeated prisoner's dilemma.

As we saw in the previous chapter, mutual cooperation can

emerge in a prisoner's dilemma only if the players believe there is a good chance they will have the opportunity to play the same game again. But in the type of situation examined here, neither player has any reason to believe that he will have a chance to play the same prisoner's dilemma game again. On the contrary, both players believe the opposite—that they will not play the same prisoner's dilemma game again.

In the type of situation studied here, the extremists on both sides are determined to pursue a radical course of action in the short run. Unwilling to compromise, the extreme left rejects gradualism. The only peaceful agreement it is willing to accept is one that would enact a broad program of radical reforms. Otherwise, the extremists of the left plan to use nondemocratic means to achieve their revolutionary ends. Because a left-leaning government is in place, leftist radicals see in the political situation a unique historical opportunity to seize power and effect a radical transformation of the country. On the other side, the extremists of the right are equally unwilling to compromise. They are determined to block reforms, so their strategy is to force the moderate right to join them in staging a military coup to oust the government and eliminate the radicals of the left. Because a left-leaning government is in place, the extremists of the right believe that, unless they quickly oust the government, the radicals will stage a leftist revolution.

Since the moderates prefer to implement a program of gradual reforms within a democratic framework, initially their problem is to find a solution acceptable to all parties in the conflict. Each moderate side has to find a solution that will please both its extremist ally and the other moderate side. The moderate left has to propose a program of reforms that is close to the radical proposals of the extreme left yet is also acceptable to the moderates of the right. On the other hand, the moderate right has to propose a program that is close to the token reforms proposed by the extreme right yet is also acceptable to the moderates of the left. Once it becomes clear that the extremists will not compromise, however, the moderates realize they cannot find a solution that includes their radical allies.

One might think that the moderates would then ignore the extremists and negotiate a plan for reforms among themselves. But they cannot do so. As I have previously explained, as long as the moderates do not break definitively with the extremists, they have good reason to fear each other and to refuse to cooperate. Thus, unless each moderate side breaks with its extremist ally, the moderates will fail to reach an agreement on reforms. As I have discussed at length, however, neither moderate side can break with its ally without losing the game. Therefore, each moderate side knows that negotiations on reform will break down and no agreement will be reached; they know that mutual cooperation is not possible.

It may be argued, of course, that, after their first failure to reach an agreement, both moderate sides might just wait for another opportunity to negotiate a settlement on reforms—that is, for another chance to play the same game again. But neither side has any reason to believe that the other will cooperate in the near future, because neither one can afford to break with its extremist ally.

Even more important, waiting for another opportunity would be too dangerous a course of action to contemplate. As we saw, each moderate side has good reason to fear that the other is conspiring with its extremist ally to seize power by force. The moderate right knows that the moderate left cannot accept the prospect of no reforms in the near future. Moderate rightists know, therefore, that the moderate left will not passively wait for another opportunity to negotiate, an opportunity the leftists do not believe in anyway. Rightly so, the moderate right fears that the moderate left will not resist the temptation to join the radicals in an attempt to get its way. By the same token, the moderate left knows that the moderate right will not risk a passive strategy when so much is at stake. Thus fearing each other, both moderate groups are likely to join the extremists to prepare themselves for the coming struggle to seize power. Moreover, since each moderate side knows that it is to the advantage of the other side to prepare for confrontation before it does, each one of them will want to join its extremist ally as quickly as possible.

All of this means that the moderates know that the prisoner's dilemma they are playing will end in mutual defection and thereafter become a zero-sum game between a united left and a united right. Both moderate sides thus believe they will not have a chance to play the same prisoner's dilemma again. As it becomes perfectly clear that the extremists will not compromise, the moderates will reject each other's proposals for reform and join their extremist allies to prepare for the eventual showdown that will put an end to democracy. Although the final showdown may not occur immediately after negotiations collapse, the situation then will no longer be one in which cooperation is an option under consideration by the moderates. The moderates will then in effect be engaging in activities aimed at seizing power by force.

This is precisely what happened in the Brazilian and Chilean cases. In both cases, when it became clear that the extremists were not going to compromise, the moderates saw that they were caught in a prisoner's dilemma, rejected each other's proposals for gradual reform, and joined their extremist allies. The resulting confrontation led to the collapse of democracy and the inauguration of an authoritarian regime. As I will show in the next two chapters, both the Brazilian and the Chilean cases unfold along the following lines. A left-leaning president about to take office meets a serious threat from the right to block his accession to power. The president manages to overcome this threat and consolidate his power. In doing so, the president strengthens the power of the extreme left, whose support is essential to consolidating his power.

Once this first crisis ends, the president and the moderates of the left negotiate with the moderates of the right to try to enact a comprehensive program of social reforms. Since they want to maintain their ties to their more radical allies, both moderate groups attempt to find a solution that is also acceptable to the extremists. Because the extremists believe they can get their way, they refuse to compromise and do everything they can to undermine the moderates' attempts to settle on a piecemeal program of reforms. Given that the extremists are unwilling to compromise, the moderates find themselves in the prisoner's dilemma situation described in this chapter. They now have to choose: either they line up with the extremists for a confrontation between left and right, or they unite and jointly attack the extremists.

The moderates also realize they will not play this same game again; once they make a choice, the situation will change radically. They know that, should they join forces, they will neutralize the extremists, implement gradual reforms, and preserve democratic institutions. But if they cannot join forces, they will have to join the extremists, and the game will turn into one of pure conflict between the left and the right, leading, one way or another, to the collapse of democracy. Unfortunately, however, the moderates cannot join forces because, as explained in this chapter and shown in the next two, each moderate side stands to lose the game by breaking with its extremist ally. Consequently, in both Brazil and Chile, the prisoner's dilemma situation ends with the moderates failing to reach an agreement on reforms. They then join their respective extremist allies and engage in a confrontational course of action which eventually leads to the demise of democracy.

Structural Explanation Revisited

I have previously argued that the kind of explanation I advance in this chapter is radically different from structural forms of explanation. One could still object, however, that I have only elaborated in greater detail what still is fundamentally a structural explanation. After all, it might be said, I have shown how the interaction between different actors constrained by their structural situation would inevitably lead to the collapse of the democratic regime. Thus conceived, my explanation would ultimately be a structural one. The only difference would perhaps reside in my greater precision in specifying the causal mechanism leading to the breakdown, which I would have achieved by resorting to game theory.

But this is far from being the case. Although my game-theoretic analysis does show that the collapse of democratic institutions was bound to happen, it does so by adducing to very different reasons than those offered by the structural explanations I criticize. Whereas structuralists claim that structural variables determined the actors' behavior and the ultimate collapse of democracy, my argument is that their beliefs and preferences did so. In other words, I argue that, *given the actors' beliefs and preferences,* they were involved in a prisoner's dilemma which resulted in the breakdown of the democratic regime. This argument can be reconciled with a structuralist perspective only if one assumes that structural conditions *determine* the beliefs and preferences of social actors.

As I have argued before, however, there are no compelling reasons to accept this assumption. Moreover, in the particular cases studied here, this does not seem to be the case at all. As far as I can see, no set of structural conditions can alone explain why groups of the left and the right chose to adopt radical courses of action in the sixties in Latin America. The radicals were by no means compelled to radicalize by the structural situation of the sixties. They could have preferred a moderate strategy, as the majority did, in which case piecemeal reforms would have been possible and the collapse of democracy would not have occurred. Similarly, if the two moderate camps had had more similar preferences for a genuine centrist alternative, they would have isolated the extremists in the first place, and the collapse would not have happened.

This does not mean that structural conditions do not play a role. They do, but only in narrowing the range of choices available to actors in a given situation. To give an example, the moderates of the right were clearly constrained by large landowners, who were among the most powerful elements of their constituency. They were thus limited by the interests of landowners in the kind of agrarian reforms they could propose. Within those limits, however, they could choose among a wide range of projects of reforms, varying from a rabidly conservative to a more progressive position. The majority of moderates at the right chose the latter, while the minority of extremists opposed reforms of any kind.

It is thus necessary to know the actors' beliefs and preferences to explain their choices, and to analyze in detail the logic of their strategic interaction, before one can provide an explanation of the final outcome. To analyze structural constraints is only to begin an explanation. In this sense, structuralists believe they have completed their task, when in effect they have merely begun.

6 BREAKDOWN BEFORE REFORMS: BRAZIL

Throughout 1963, social reform was at the center of the political turmoil that overtook Brazilian society. In the beginning there was much hope that Congress would pass legislation enacting major social, political, and economic changes. As the year took its course, however, Congress failed to pass the reforms, political conflict intensified, and the military intervened. Before any reforms were enacted, the democratic regime collapsed in March of 1964. The purpose of this chapter is to explain why this occurred. I will show that the breakdown of Brazilian democracy was the outcome of a political conflict over reforms that took the shape of the prisoner's dilemma described in the previous chapter of this book.

Introduction to the Brazilian Case

Brazilian democracy had lasted for two decades before it collapsed in March of 1964.[1] It collapsed during the term of President Goulart, who had succeeded Jânio Quadros when he resigned in August of 1961.[2] At the time of Quadros's resignation, Goulart was vice president, which entitled him to assume the presidency. In spite of his constitutional right to do so, the three military ministers of Quadros's government and powerful civilian right-wingers attempted to block his accession to the presidency.[3]

Goulart was a populist politician of the Labor Party (PTB—Partido Trabalhista Brasileiro) who had strong ties to the left.[4] His association with the left and his advocacy of sweeping social, economic, and political reforms frightened the military as well as civilians from both the center and the extreme right. Nevertheless, the overwhelming majority of congressmen and a significant number of military officers were unwilling to go against constitutional stipulations for presidential succession.[5] After much skirmishing, those who favored Goulart's accession and those who were against it reached an agreement. Goulart would assume the presidency, but he would rule under a parliamentary rather than a presidential system.

The turn to parliamentarism in August of 1961 was a deliberate attempt to prevent Goulart from implementing his radical program of "basic reforms."[6] The parliamentary system greatly increased the power of Congress over the president.[7] Since the leading party in Congress, the PSD (Partido Social Democrático), was a center-right party that favored only a piecemeal program of reforms, the parliamentary system ensured that reforms would be implemented in a very gradual manner.[8]

The effort to contain Goulart and the left through a parliamentary regime was ultimately unsuccessful. It failed not only because Goulart and the left mounted an effective campaign against parliamentarism but also because many influential politicians were not really committed to a parliamentary form of government.[9] Prominent politicians who had a chance to win the presidential elections of 1965 did not want to rule under a parliamentary system. Neither did current and aspiring state governors, who feared parliamentarism would eventually be extended to the states. And many congressmen were against parliamentarism because they feared it was unpopular, which would put them at great risk in the approaching congressional elections of October 1962.

All of these politicians had originally supported parliamentarism as an expedient way of solving the crisis caused by Quadros's resignation. They had been willing to adopt the parliamentary regime on a temporary basis, only on the condition that it be submitted to a referendum nine months before the end of Goulart's term, in 1965.[10] As the congressional elections neared, however, congressmen who feared parliamentarism was unpopular began to campaign for an early return to the presidential system. The antiparliamentary coalition finally got its way when Congress approved a bill to move the plebiscite on parliamentarism to an earlier date. On January 6, 1963, Brazilians voted five to one for a return to the presidential regime.[11]

As soon as Goulart regained full presidential powers, the radical program of "basic reforms" was thrust with full force onto the political agenda, creating a political crisis far more severe than the one preceding it. This crisis could be solved only if the moderates in Congress reached an agreement on the implementation of a program of reforms. As we shall see, however, such an agreement was never reached because the moderates were caught in a prisoner's dilemma. Ultimately, the failure to reach an agreement in Congress precipitated the events that led to the collapse of the democratic regime in 1964.

The Possibility of Reform

Structuralists have argued that the Brazilian Congress failed to pass major reforms because the majority of congressmen were conservative representatives of the dominant classes.[12] These congressmen would have voted against reforms because they were against the interests of the classes they represented. Yet the brunt of the evidence suggests otherwise. At the start of 1963, the great majority of Congress was in favor of, if not radical reforms, at least a piecemeal program of reforms. A survey conducted by a major newspaper from Rio de Janeiro, *Correio da Manhã,* showed that more than 70 percent of the representatives were favorable to at least a moderate program of reforms.[13] Since in 1963 the left parties had about 40 percent of the seats in the Chamber of Deputies, the survey indicated that more than half of the more conservative representatives favored a piecemeal program of reforms.[14]

Most of these were from the center-right PSD, the leading party in Congress with 29 percent of the seats in the Chamber of Deputies and 36 percent of the seats in the Senate.[15] The moderate politicians of the PSD had long decided that major reforms, like the agrarian reform, were both necessary and inevitable.[16] If the PSD were to survive politically, they reasoned, it would have to support a program of reforms. The main objective of the PSD should therefore not be to oppose the widespread demand for reforms but rather to domesticate it through the implementation of a piecemeal and gradual program of reforms. Thus, in spite of much protest from its constituency of landowners, the PSD in 1962 had officially pronounced itself in favor of reforms.[17]

In March of 1962, the Ninth National Convention of the PSD had issued the Declaration of Brasília, which defined the party's position on reforms.[18] The declaration made a major concession to the left concerning compensation for the expropriation of unproductive land. According to the Constitution of 1946, expropriations had to be compensated in cash, and cash compensations would obviously greatly limit the scope of any land reform. This provision of the Constitution had prompted the left to advocate a constitutional amendment allowing compensations to be paid in public bonds. By agreeing to an amendment that would allow for compensation in public bonds rather than cash, the PSD's Declaration of Brasília went a long way toward meeting the demands of the left.

The right's support for piecemeal reform was by no means confined to the PSD. Even among the more extreme right-wing congressmen of the UDN (União Democrática Nacional) there was considerable support for moderate agrarian reform. The UDN had a progressive wing of representatives known as the "Bossa Nova" who were supportive of agrarian reform.[19] Even though the Bossa Nova was a minority within the UDN, in early 1963 the majority of UDN congressmen were leaning toward this progressive wing of their party.[20] It was only later in the year that the reactionary wing led by Carlos Lacerda managed to seize the leadership of the UDN.[21]

At the outset of 1963, then, a piecemeal, though substantial, program of reforms had a good chance of being passed by Congress. The PSD had agreed to pass the most important piece of legislation—the amendment allowing for compensation of expropriated land in public bonds—necessary to the effective implementation of an agrarian reform. Since Goulart's party, the PTB, and the other parties of the left controlled 40 percent of the seats in the Chamber of Deputies and the PSD 29 percent, together they had more than the two-thirds of the votes required to pass a constitutional amendment.[22] In all likelihood, an amendment supported by the PSD could have received even more votes, given that a substantial number of representatives in the UDN and other parties of the right were willing to support a program of piecemeal reforms backed by the leading party (PSD).

The problem, of course, lay in reconciling the differences between Goulart and the PTB, on the one hand, and the PSD, on the other. Though both groups agreed on the need for an amendment allowing for compensation in public bonds, they disagreed on the rate of adjustment to inflation that should be applied to these bonds, as well as on the criteria by which land could be expropriated.[23] Compared to Goulart and the PTB, the PSD wanted a considerably higher correction for inflation, and criteria of expropriation that would more severely limit its amount and scope. Important as they were, those differences were far from irreconcilable.[24]

At the beginning of 1963, both Goulart and the PSD had much to gain from reaching an agreement on a program of agrarian and other reforms. Though Goulart, the leader of the PTB, had used the radical left for his own political purposes, he was far from being a radical himself.[25] Goulart was eager to become the first president to implement major reforms, and the prospect of having Congress pass the first constitutional amendment for that purpose was extremely attractive to him. As for their part, the leaders of the PSD felt that they could maintain their leading electoral position only if they supported the implementation of a substantial, though piecemeal, program of agrarian and other reforms.[26]

It is true, however, that both Goulart and the leaders of the PSD would have to contend with the minority of radicals in their coalitions if they were to meet halfway on the issue of agrarian reform. Neither the small minority of radical leftists led by Leonel Brizola nor that of right-wing extremists led by Carlos Lacerda were willing to compromise.[27] Nevertheless, these groups were too small a minority to jeopardize an agreement between the PTB and the PSD. The radicals of both the left and the right could matter only if the overwhelming majority of moderates and their leaders allowed them to prosper.

The Moderates' Dilemma

If the moderates of the right and the left were willing to reach an agreement on agrarian reform, stood to gain from it, and had the means to turn it into legislation, what explains their failure to reach such an agreement? If, at the beginning of 1963, both sides stood to benefit from agreeing on a program of agrarian reform, why is it that by October they had rejected each other's proposals, thereby destroying all chances of an agreement between them?

My answer is that the two moderate sides could not reach an agreement because they were suspicious of each other's ultimate intentions. Each side suspected the other would use its radical allies to impose its will on the other. As long as the moderates maintained their relations with the radicals, each moderate side felt fundamentally threatened by the other. The PSD feared that Goulart and the PTB, with support from the extreme left, might eventually impose unacceptable changes of a radical nature, while Goulart and the PTB feared that the PSD, backed by the extreme right and the military, would trick them into accepting a meaningless program of reforms, if not worse.[28] Thus, they could not reach an agreement on major reforms unless each side unambiguously and irreversibly broke its ties with the radicals.

As we shall see, however, neither moderate side could break with its extremist counterpart. This was the case because each side stood to gain more from maintaining its ties to the radicals no matter what the other side did. The two moderate sides were involved in a prisoner's dilemma game in which the rational strategy for each side was to maintain its ties with the extremists in its own camp. Thus, neither side could act to dispel the suspicions of the other, which meant that no agreement on agrarian and other major reforms could be reached.

Mutual Suspicions

As we saw, the moderate rightists of the PSD and the UDN were willing to vote for a piecemeal program of reforms, even if that meant passing the constitutional amendment for agrarian reform. But they were reluctant to do so because of the strong ties Goulart and the PTB maintained with the radical left.[29]

Although still a small minority in the PTB and in Congress, the radical leftists had grown to be a significant power in Brazilian society.[30] Leonel Brizola, Goulart's brother-in-law and the leader of the radicals in the PTB, was an extremely popular politician in the major urban centers of the country. And the radicals outside Congress had made substantial inroads in the labor movement. Members of this Jacobin left could be found in peak labor organizations, such as the CGT (Comando Geral dos Trabalhadores), the CGC (Comando Geral de Greve) and the PUA

(Pacto Sindical de Unidade e Ação); in the Brazilian Communist Party (PCB) and its pro-Chinese splinter, the Communist Party of Brazil (PC do B); in the main organs of the official corporative labor structure, the bureaucracy of the Ministry of Labor, and the social security institutes; in the Peasant Leagues of Francisco Juliao; and in the major student movement organizations, such as the UNE (União Nacional dos Estudantes) and the Roman Catholic AP (Ação Popular).

Though Goulart was not himself a radical, and both he and the radicals were uneasy about their alliance, they both profited from their symbiotic relationship.[31] Goulart had built a career out of helping the radicals to gain power within the corporative labor bureaucracy controlled by the Ministry of Labor. The radicals returned the favor by organizing rallies, demonstrations, and strikes that helped Goulart to achieve his own political purposes. Goulart had relied on the radical leftists as early as 1953, during his brief tenure as Vargas's minister of labor, and had benefited from their help both in overcoming the military's reluctance to let him succeed Quadros in 1961 and in pressuring Congress to allow him to regain full presidential powers before the legally stipulated date. By 1963, Goulart's tactics had earned him a reputation for being an opportunistic agitator who rarely hesitated to manipulate mass discontent for his own personal gain.

Thus, the moderates of the right had good reason to fear that Goulart and the PTB would again use the radical left to pressure them and the Congress into unacceptably radical reforms. They feared that, in this way, Goulart would turn every concession into an opportunity to extract further concessions from the right, until he got his way. As the right-wingers from the UDN never ceased to remind them, moderate rightists suspected Goulart's ultimate intention was to rule dictatorially in the manner of Vargas or Peron.[32] Goulart's campaign for agrarian reform would be his first step toward achieving that goal. Passing a constitutional amendment enabling agrarian reform would increase Goulart's popularity and create an atmosphere conducive to other reforms, which would further increase his popularity and power, and so on, until Goulart and the left would reign supreme.

Among these other reforms, the most threatening were two prospective amendments, one allowing Goulart to be reelected in 1965 (the Constitution prohibited presidential reelection), and one enfranchising illiterates, which would double the electorate to the advantage of Goulart and the left.[33] Before 1963, Goulart had repeatedly tried to circumvent the two-thirds vote required to pass these amendments by maneuvering to include them in broader bills requiring only a simple majority of votes.[34] Thus, the moderate rightists had reason to fear that Goulart would continue to pursue those goals with the help of his radical friends. Such a prospect generated deep apprehension within the right, since many believed that, if Goulart could institute all of these changes in the electoral rules, it would be virtually impossible to stop him from establishing a popular dictatorship of the left.

Given Goulart's record, then, it is not surprising that the leaders of the PSD—as willing as they were to reach an agreement with Goulart and his party (PTB)—were extremely reluctant to do so unless the president took a clear stand against the projects, strategies, and tactics of the radical leftists. Goulart had to show that he was willing to forgo support from the radicals, and even to take action against them if necessary, before the PSD moderates could believe he would not take advantage of the major concessions they were about to make. The moderates of the right knew, and the extremist right-wingers constantly reminded them, that Goulart and the moderates of the left had very strong incentives to use the Jacobin left to extract further concessions until they irreversibly tilted the balance of power in their favor. So the moderates of the PSD had to be assured that Goulart could no longer resort to the Jacobin left before they agreed to implement major reforms. This could happen only if Goulart forcefully severed his relations with the extremists of the left.[35]

Moderate congressmen repeatedly asked Goulart to make this break. Even as late as mid-1963, when the first round of negotiations on reforms had failed, Goulart's attempts to stabilize the economy had been unsuccessful, and the situation had further radicalized, congressmen from the PSD were still demanding that Goulart repudiate Brizola's attacks on Congress.[36] They were joined by the moderate press and by moderate officers, who cautioned Goulart to dissociate himself from the attacks of radical leftists against powerful conservative officers and from "Brizola's collusion with radical leftist organizers among the noncommissioned ranks."[37] Even some of the moderates within the PTB cautioned Goulart. As the leader of the "positive left," San

Tiago Dantas, resigned his position as finance minister in June of 1963, he wrote Goulart cautioning him against "the less responsible left led by Brizola," which he believed was jeopardizing negotiations for a moderate program of reforms.[38]

But Goulart and the moderates of the PTB were equally suspicious of the moderate right. Although the leaders of the PSD had always been careful to avoid any open association with the right-wingers of the UDN, many of its most conservative members disliked Goulart and maintained close connections with the extreme right in case it became necessary to take concerted action against his Caesarist ambitions.[39] Goulart knew, as everyone else did, that the shrewd PSD politicians would do anything in their power to keep reforms to a minimum. Goulart also feared that many politicians of the PSD were covertly conspiring with the extreme right and its military allies to undermine his ambition to become the major leader who had brought "basic reforms" to Brazil.[40] Goulart repeatedly expressed these suspicions and fears when he justified his refusal to abandon the radicals, arguing that he would then "become easy prey to the conservatives—or worse."[41]

Thus, without mutual reassurance in the form of a repudiation of their radical allies, the moderates of the left and the right could not possibly reach an agreement on the agrarian or any other major reform. But neither moderate side could break with its radical ally because, as I have already said, they were involved in a prisoner's dilemma: no matter what the other side did, each moderate side stood to gain the most by not breaking relations with its radical ally. To show that this was the case, I will now analyze in turn the situation faced by each of the moderate sides.

The Defection of the Moderate Left

Goulart and the moderates of his party had two options: to break with Brizola and the Jacobins or to maintain their alliance with them. Let us analyze the consequences of each choice in turn.

If Goulart seriously broke with the radicals—which meant that he would have to be ready to take severe action against them should they continue to radicalize the situation—he would be able to reap the substantial rewards of an agreement with the PSD—that is, if the PSD decided to cooperate. In the parlance of the prisoner's dilemma (see figs. 3 and 4), Goulart and the PTB would then receive the payoff *R,* the reward for cooperation.

As we saw, the moderate right also stood to gain by cooperating with Goulart. If Goulart broke with the radicals, however, the PSD stood to gain even more by maintaining its relations with the extreme right and its military allies. The PSD could then threaten a vulnerable Goulart into accepting as minimal a program of reforms as possible. Even if the PSD agreed to vote for an agrarian reform amendment allowing for compensation in public bonds, it could still force a weakened Goulart and his party to accept an extremely limited program of agrarian and other reforms. But it was also conceivable that, given the fact that Goulart could no longer rely on his radical friends, the PSD would no longer have an incentive to uphold its promise to support the constitutional amendment.[42]

Thus, if Goulart decided to break with his radical allies, and the PSD decided to maintain its relations with its own, he would end his term as a mediocre ruler, who not only had betrayed his leftist allies but also had been unsuccessful in implementing even a moderate program of reforms.[43] In the language of the prisoner's dilemma, if he severed his ties to the radical left, he would have ended up collecting his worst payoff, *S,* the sucker's payoff.

On the other hand, if Goulart and the PTB decided to maintain their alliance with the Jacobins, they could secure better outcomes. If the PSD cooperated, taking a firm stance in favor of the left and against the extreme right, the threat of a military coup would no longer be credible. The great majority of the Brazilian military would not intervene without strong civilian backing.[44] Goulart and his radical allies could then force the weakened moderate rightists to accept a far broader program of reforms. This outcome would give the moderate left its best payoff—*T,* the temptation to defect.

If the PSD refused to cooperate, then there would be a confrontation between a unified left and a cohesive right. A confrontation would give Goulart and the moderate left the payoff *P,* the punishment for defection.

Goulart and the moderate left preferred reaching a peaceful agreement with the PSD to a confrontation (that is, they preferred *R* to *P*) because the latter was a risky affair: it was possible that a confrontation would lead to defeat. But they preferred a confrontation to the sucker's payoff (that is, P to S) because they believed they had an excellent chance of mobilizing considerable popular support to pressure Congress into passing their program of reform before the military would intervene.[45] As we shall see, Goulart, the moderate left, and the radicals overestimated their capacity to do so.[46] But before the confrontation actually took place, they believed it would work in their favor.

It is clear, then, that the rank ordering of the payoffs for the moderate left was that of the prisoner's dilemma game: $T > R > P > S$. Given that their payoffs for maintaining their alliance with the radicals were greater than their payoffs for breaking it, no matter what the other side did, the moderate leftists stood to gain more by keeping their ties to Brizola and the Jacobins. Thus, in 1963, Goulart and the PTB chose to maintain their alliance with the radicals of the left.

The Defection of the Moderate Right

As the leading party of the center, the PSD had traditionally avoided any open support either of the extreme right or of military intervention. But its position toward Goulart was at best ambivalent, if not negative, and the moderate rightists of the PSD kept in close touch with the extremists of the UDN in case Goulart and the left decided on a more radical course of action.[47]

To reassure Goulart and the PTB, however, the PSD would have to do better than hedge its bets. It would have to show a far more favorable face to Goulart and take a stronger stance against the extremists of the right.[48] It would also have to repudiate unambiguously any attempt at military intervention. In short, the PSD also had two options: it either repudiated the extremists or continued to uphold its "neutrality," leaving open a potential alliance with the extreme right and their military allies.

If the leaders of the PSD unambiguously took a stand against the extreme right, and the moderates of the left broke with their radical allies, they would be able to reach an agreement on reforms. This was an attractive outcome to them, as we saw, because it would preserve democratic institutions and yield considerable electoral dividends to the PSD. Thus if they repudiated the extremists, and the moderate left did the same, they would reap R, the reward for cooperation.

As we saw earlier, however, Goulart and the PTB stood to gain even more from keeping their allies if the PSD decided to turn against theirs. The PSD would then lose its capacity to threaten the left into compliance, which would enable Goulart and his radical allies to impose a far more radical program of reforms—or worse.[49] In this case, the PSD, and the other moderate rightists, would collect *S*, the sucker's payoff.

On the other hand, if the PSD left open the possibility for an alliance with the extreme right and its military allies, it could secure far better outcomes. For in this case, if the moderates of the left decided to repudiate the Jacobins, the moderates of the right would be in a position to impose a more limited program of reforms within the boundaries of a democratic system. And the left would be considerably weakened. This outcome would give the PSD its best payoff—*T*, the temptation to defect.

Should Goulart and the PTB also maintain their radical allies, there would be an all-out confrontation. The PSD would then collect *P*, the punishment for defection.

Although the moderates of the PSD much preferred reaching a peaceful agreement to a confrontation (*R* to *P*) because the latter could lead to the breakdown of democracy and a loss of their leading electoral position, they certainly preferred a confrontation to letting the left have its radical way (*P* to *S*). The PSD was intent on preventing a radical transformation of Brazilian society, and it was confident that with the help of the UDN and the military a confrontation would result in a victory against the left.[50]

It is thus evident that the ranking of the payoffs for the moderate right was also that of the prisoner's dilemma game: $T > R > P > S$. Whatever actions the other side took, the PSD stood to gain by maintaining its potential alliance with the UDN extremists and their military friends.

The Failure to Reach an Agreement

Since neither moderate side ever broke off its relations with its radical counterpart, no agreement on a program of agrarian reform was reached. Negotiations in Congress began in April 1963. Within six months, an agreement on agrarian reforms was virtually impossible.

Though not negligible, the disagreements between the PTB

and the PSD were hardly fundamental. The parties agreed on the most important issue—the need for a constitutional amendment permitting the government to pay for expropriated land in public bonds. The disagreements focused on the rate at which the bonds would be corrected for inflation, the criteria by which rural property would be expropriated, and the extension of expropriation to urban property.[51]

On the first issue, the PSD proposed a correction of 30 percent to 50 percent instead of the 10 percent proposed by the PTB. As to the criteria for expropriation of rural property, the PSD wanted to set more stringent limits than those proposed by the PTB. The PSD's amendment proposal exempted two types of rural property from expropriation: those of less than five hundred hectares and located more than fifty kilometers from cities with at least 50,000 inhabitants, and those that exploited 50 percent or more of their area. In addition, of those lands that could be expropriated, the owners could retain as much as half of their property, up to five hundred hectares. The PSD's proposal also included a formula to determine whether any given rural property showed "satisfactory economic exploitation," which would exempt it from expropriation. Basically, the idea was that, to be expropriable, a rural property had to achieve a level of productivity equal to the average productivity of other properties in the region operating under similar conditions of climate and soil.

These two disagreements could be more easily reconciled than the third. This last disagreement involved the expropriation of urban property. Whereas the PTB's proposed amendment allowed for the expropriation of urban property, the PSD claimed such expropriation should not be part of the plan for agrarian reform.[52] Although this was a controversial issue, the expropriation of urban property was definitely not essential to Goulart's and the PTB's plan of agrarian reform. They could have compromised easily on this issue in exchange for concessions that were far more central to their plan. Given the severe consequences that a confrontation might entail, as opposed to the substantial rewards an agreement could bring, and the lack of disagreement on fundamental issues, one would have expected the parties to meet each other halfway. But the atmosphere of suspicion and radicalization in which the negotiations were conducted precluded that outcome.

From the very start, both sides did nothing to reassure each other. On the contrary, Goulart and the PTB deepened the suspicions of the moderate rightists by including the expropriation of urban property in their amendment proposal.[53] Although the matter was clearly open to negotiation, the proposal's obvious association with the radical left alarmed the PSD. Rather than repudiating the Jacobins, Goulart and the PTB were including them in the negotiations. Predictably, such an inclusion reinforced the fears of the moderates of the PSD, thereby decreasing their willingness to compromise. Even worse, from the very start the negotiations on agrarian reform were accompanied by disruptive actions from radicals of both the left and the right.[54] Brizola and the Jacobins initiated a tumultuous campaign to pressure Congress into compliance. They continually threatened to resort to extraparliamentary action in case the "reactionary" Congress did not pass the left's proposals, while the extreme right-wingers of the UDN hurled the usual public invectives against the "subversive" nature of Goulart and the left's reforms.

Since neither Goulart nor the leaders of the PSD did much to repudiate the radicals and to reassure each other, negotiations quickly reached an impasse. By August of 1963 the leaders of the moderates of both the left and the right had rejected flat out each other's proposals for an agrarian reform amendment. None of these proposals would receive the required two-thirds vote were they to be submitted to the floor of Congress.[55] At this point it had become clear that an agreement on agrarian reform could no longer be reached. Even many moderates in the PSD—especially the representatives from Minas Gerais and the center of the country—had joined the UDN in its attempt to prevent any constitutional reform from passing in Congress.[56]

Nevertheless, the PTB insisted on submitting its proposal to a vote in Congress. Hostilities had reached such a level as to prompt the PTB and the Jacobins to force the moderates of the right to reject the left's proposal for reform. They thought that by doing so they would expose the allegedly reactionary character of a Congress that was unwilling to pass even a very limited set of reforms.[57] The amendment proposed by the PTB, and endorsed by Goulart, was finally rejected in October of 1963 by 60 percent of the 283 congressmen who voted on the proposal.[58]

Confrontation and Collapse

By October, the political situation had already radicalized to the point where any future agreement on agrarian reform was virtually impossible. Although the moderates on both sides had not yet completely sided with their respective extremist allies, many among them had increasingly become reluctant to compromise. After the proposals for reform were all rejected, the situation turned more and more to one of confrontation between the left and the right.

The Strategy of the Extremists

The extremists of both the left and the right had played a major role in radicalizing the situation. Neither group of extremists wanted the moderates to reach an agreement to pass a piecemeal and gradual program of reforms. On the contrary, both wanted to split the moderates and drive them into a more radical course of action. The extremists of the right wanted the PSD moderates to join them in blocking reforms in Congress or in persuading the military to oust Goulart. The radical leftists wanted Goulart and the PTB to join them in forcing Congress to pass radical reforms, or, short of this, to impose these radical changes by extraconstitutional means.

To split the moderates and to drive them toward a more radical course of action, the strategy of the extremists was to play on both the fear the moderates had of each other and the fear each moderate side had of losing support from its extremist allies and other members within its own constituencies. As I explained in chapter 5, the extremists played on these fears by attacking the moderates whenever they showed any willingness to cooperate with or make concessions to each other. The radical leftists attacked the moderate leftists, accusing them of caving in to the "reactionary" demands of the right, while the extremist rightwingers attacked the moderate rightists, accusing them of caving in to the demands of the radicals. These attacks ultimately forced the moderates to back away from their initial concessions in an attempt to accommodate their extremist allies. In doing so, however, each moderate side reinforced the other's suspicion that it was in fact colluding with its extremist allies.

Playing on the suspicions of the moderates, and feeding off each other's radical activities, the extremists were able to set in motion a spiral of radicalization which drove the moderates apart and ultimately led to the all-out confrontation that resulted in the military coup of 1964.

Using these divisive tactics, the extremists seized every opportunity they had to split the moderates apart and to radicalize the situation. As we saw, the extremists of both the left and the right did their very best to jeopardize the negotiations on agrarian reform between the two moderate parties in Congress.[59] Led by Brizola, the radical leftists mounted an aggressive campaign denouncing the negotiations in Congress as a "reactionary" ploy to curtail genuine reform. They vowed to resort to extraparliamentary action in the event that Congress did not pass their radical reforms, and threatened to withdraw support from Goulart if he caved in to the demands of the right. On the other side, Lac erda and the right-wingers of the UDN used similar tactics, denouncing the negotiations as a "subversive" ploy to pass radical reforms. The extremists thus reinforced the mutual fears of the moderates, splitting them apart on the issue of agrarian reform.

The radicals of both the left and the right also seized the opportunity afforded by Goulart's policies of economic stabilization to promote dissension among the moderates, thereby aggravating the polarization generated by the issue of agrarian reform. Economic stabilization, like agrarian reform, was part of the Dantas-Furtado Three-Year Plan.[60] Adopted by Goulart early in 1963, the Three-Year Plan was designed to turn around the deteriorating economic situation. Its main objectives were to reduce inflation without jeopardizing economic growth, and to implement structural and institutional reforms to remove obstacles to economic development. Inflation would be curbed through wage restraint, cuts in government expenditures, credit tightening, and ceilings on prices. With these stabilization measures, the government hoped to please the U.S. government and the IMF so as to secure financial aid and the rescheduling and financing of the

Brazilian foreign debt. As far as reforms were concerned, the plan included administrative, banking, and tax reforms as well as changes in the agrarian structure of the country.

Since the radicals of both the left and the right had no interest in a compromise between the moderates, they both attacked the Three-Year Plan.[61] Both sides organized a concerted campaign against Goulart's plan that included aggressive press releases, rallies, public demonstrations, strikes, and threats of major strikes. Led by Brizola, the radical left denounced the plan for being halfhearted where reforms were concerned, maintaining that its real goal was to appease the "reactionaries" in Congress, the capitalists and the imperialist powers. On the other side, the right-wingers led by Lacerda claimed that the plan's stabilization measures were weak, and that its true goal was to impose revolutionary changes involving the redistribution of wealth, power, and property. Together, the extremists successfully played on the fears of the moderates, who subsequently withdrew their support from the plan, thus forcing Goulart to abandon his attempt to stabilize the economy.

The same radicalizing tactics were again used by the radicals when in April of 1963 the government announced its intention to purchase the American and Foreign Power Company (AMFORP) for $135 million, 75 percent of which would be reinvested in nonutility enterprises in Brazil.[62] The government was anxious to purchase the company as soon as possible, since three of its subsidiaries had been the target of expropriations by state governments.[63] To prevent further incidents of this sort, and to avoid retaliation from the U.S. government, Goulart had agreed to purchase U.S.-owned public utilities on condition that the funds from the sale would be reinvested in manufacturing industries in Brazil.

The extremists of the left did not lose any time in attacking the planned purchase of AMFORP. Leading the attack from the left, Brizola predictably accused the government of engaging in a "sellout." He attacked every aspect of the government's policy, demanding higher wage settlements, confiscation of foreign companies with minimal compensation, and more radical reforms. As Skidmore puts it, Brizola and the radical left took center stage, "attacking the 'entreguistas' around the President, the 'reactionaries' in Congress, the 'gorillas' in the Army, and the 'imperialists' in the American Embassy and the IMF."[64] Brizola's outburst prompted the usual backlash from the extreme right, but it also alarmed the moderates from every quarter, who again asked the president and the PTB to repudiate the radical left.

But Goulart did not take a firm stand against the radical left. His continued refusal to do so, even in the face of mounting radicalization, frightened the moderates of the right and further jeopardized the chances for an agreement on agrarian reforms. By the middle of 1963, the moderates of the UDN had closed ranks with the radical wing of their party, and influential moderates of the PSD began to speak out against constitutional changes.[65] On the other hand, since the moderates of the PSD were moving closer to the right, the moderates of the PTB also hardened their position on agrarian reform.

This incipient polarization of the moderates was further accentuated by Goulart's reaction to an incident in September 1963—the sergeants' rebellion against the Supreme Court's decision to deny them the right to be elected for public office.[66] As a protest against the court's ruling, the sergeants seized the buildings of the ministries of justice and the navy, as well as the headquarters of the navy and air force; they arrested the acting president of the Chamber of Deputies and a minister of the Supreme Court; and they severed radio and telephone communication between Brasília and the rest of the country. The revolt was quickly subdued. But Goulart supported the sergeants' claims, arguing they were part of the program of reforms promoted by the government. This was especially alarming to the moderates of the right in view of the fact that the sergeants had been in close contact with the radical labor leaders of the CGT, who had threatened a national strike in support of the rebelling soldiers.

Even more important, however, was the effect the rebellion, and Goulart's reaction to it, had upon the moderates in the military. Legalist high-ranking officers, who were in principle against military intervention in civilian affairs, were alarmed by what they felt was a leftist attempt to disrupt military discipline from below. Goulart's unwillingness to punish the rebellious soldiers fueled their suspicions that the president and the left were sowing discord in the military and would eventually capitalize upon a divided military to stage a coup against the constitutional process. Therefore, although still unwilling to take any action against the president, senior officers began to organize a "defensive" conspiracy in the event that the president overstepped the boundaries of the constitutional order.[67]

Lacerda and his right-wing followers seized this opportunity to instigate the military to action. Lacerda went so far as to invite U.S. intervention, claiming that the "communist" and "totalitarian" Goulart was still in power because the military were hesitant to remove him.[68] Goulart's military ministers were outraged by Lacerda's attack, and issued a recriminatory statement asserting that his declarations were deliberately meant to create agitation and disorder.

In the wake of these tumultuous events of September and October, and a mounting wave of strikes, demonstrations, and incidents of political violence, Goulart's military ministers urged him to declare a state of siege.[69] They argued that emergency rule was necessary to restrain radicalization, both from the left and the right, and to restore the minimum of order required to govern the country effectively. Using Lacerda's virulent attack against the government to justify a state of siege to his friends on the left, on October 4 Goulart requested from Congress approval for rule by state of siege for thirty days. Far from restoring the moderates' confidence in Goulart, the request for emergency powers further accentuated their suspicions. The moderates of the right reasoned that, though a measure of coercion was necessary to restore order, the government already had the coercive capacity to do so. Therefore Goulart probably had ulterior motives in requesting a state of siege. As for the left, both moderates and radicals feared that they would ultimately be the targets of repression under emergency rule. Opposed by all groups, Goulart withdrew his request three days after he had submitted it to Congress.

The Collapse of the Democratic Regime

Thus, by October 7, 1963, when Congress had rejected Goulart's and the PTB's amendment for agrarian reform, a number of other issues had fueled the political polarization engendered by the debates about the reform itself. By then, the PSD moderates had good reason to suspect that Goulart would continue to rely on the radical left to achieve his political goals. Similarly, Goulart and the PTB could now see that many moderates within the PSD were aligning themselves with the right-wingers of the UDN, and that a civilian-military conspiracy to topple the government was under way. Rather than parting with the extremists, the moderates were increasingly drifting toward them. The radicals at both extremes of the political spectrum had successfully exploited the mutual fears and suspicions of the moderates, and an agreement on reforms was now almost impossible. No matter what Goulart and the leaders of the PSD did, by October of 1963 it was probably too late to reach an agreement in Congress and to avert an eventual confrontation between the left and the right.

Nevertheless, Goulart made a last attempt to force the Congress to pass a constitutional amendment for agrarian reform. In a last-ditch effort to goad the PSD into reaching an agreement on agrarian reform, he threatened to implement reforms by decree. There were a number of measures Goulart could take that did not require legislative action. Though these measures would be far less effective without a constitutional amendment allowing for compensation in public bonds, they were nevertheless threatening enough to merit attention. Thus, in December of 1963, Goulart announced his intention to put into effect what became known as the SUPRA Decree.[70] The first in a series of measures toward implementing agrarian reforms, it regulated the expropriation of landholdings close to federal highways, railways, dams, and irrigation and drainage projects.

Goulart introduced the decree merely as a warning to the PSD, since he signed it only in March 1964, when he made his final radical turn to the extreme left. Nevertheless, in spite of well-intentioned efforts by individual moderates to reconcile Goulart with the PSD, the SUPRA Decree ultimately reinforced hostilities between all parties concerned. In January 1964 the situation seemed beyond repair. To avoid the final disastrous confrontation, San Tiago Dantas, the leader of the "positive left" in the PTB, made a heroic attempt to reconstruct a coalition between the left and the PSD.[71] He formed the Progressive Front (Frente Progressista de Apoio às Reformas de Base) and negotiated tirelessly to unite the left under the dominance of the moderates. Dantas and his moderate followers of the PTB appealed to all centrist forces to rally around the government in an effort to defuse the process of radicalization and to re-create the conditions for the enactment of reforms by democratic means.

But Dantas's appeals fell on deaf ears. In early 1964, the PSD was too divided and too suspicious of Goulart's intentions to join the Front. The PTB was also divided, with many of its members now unwilling to compromise on the issue of "basic reforms." And Goulart himself was extremely reluctant to lend his support to the Front. As for the radicals on both sides, they had no interest whatsoever in avoiding a confrontation. On the contrary, leftist radicals were convinced that a confrontation would be to their advantage, while extreme right-wingers were conspiring to depose Goulart.

With the failure of the Progressive Front, the radicals finally got what they wanted. Goulart's unmistakable turn to the radical left came at a massive rally held on March 13, 1964, in Rio de Janeiro.[72] During that rally, Goulart dramatically signed the SUPRA Decree and another decree nationalizing all private oil refineries. In his speech he declared the Constitution obsolete because it stood in the way of reforms that would create a more just and humane society. Goulart also announced his intention to issue decrees implementing other reforms, and promised to propose legislation to Congress on the enfranchisement of illiterates and enlisted servicemen as well as on the legalization of the Communist party. Finally, both he and his brother-in-law Leonel Brizola made it clear that they would mobilize mass support to bypass Congress or even close it if it continued to block their program of reforms.

Between the rally of March 13 and his annual message to Congress on March 15, in which Goulart reiterated his intention to impose his project of "basic reforms," moderates among both the civilians and the military withdrew their already shaken support of the government and joined the conspirators of the right. On March 10, the PSD broke its relations with the government.[73] The military coup finally came a few days after Goulart's outright challenge of the military hierarchy during the naval mutiny of March 26, when Goulart dismissed the naval minister who attempted to quell the mutiny and allowed the CGT to choose a new minister to replace him.[74]

The radicals had succeeded in their dogged attempts to split the moderates by exploiting their fears of each other. But when the final confrontation came, Goulart and the left painfully realized that they had seriously overestimated their power to mobilize the masses in their struggle against the right.[75] Their successful mobilizations—in favor of Goulart's accession to power in 1961 and later of his resumption of full presidential powers in 1962 and 1963—had led them to exaggerate their own power.

The radical left failed to recognize that these past successes were largely due to favorable circumstances over which they had no control. As Erickson and others have shown, the radical left had not organized the masses that supported them.[76] They merely took advantage of the economic grievances of the workers and other favorable circumstances to launch strikes and demonstrations to achieve their own political goals. But their capacity to do so depended on the tolerance of the military, who, as Erickson puts it, "generally assumed a position of benevolent neutrality or active support in the period prior to 1963."[77] Thus, the "successes" of the radical left prior to 1963 were largely due to factors unrelated to their own political power. The situation changed dramatically in 1963, but Goulart and the left held to their belief that they were strong enough to impose radical changes through mass mobilization.

7 REFORMS BEFORE BREAKDOWN: CHILE

Like Goulart, Allende wanted to implement a sweeping program of socioeconomic and political reforms under a democratic regime.[1] His major goals were to extend the agrarian reform initiated in 1962 by the Alessandri government, to redistribute income in favor of workers, to nationalize foreign industries, and to expand state ownership and control of the economy. The socialist president also wanted Congress to pass a constitutional amendment that would strengthen the presidency by instituting a new unicameral legislature to be elected simultaneously with the president for a six-year term.

Unlike Goulart, however, Allende came to power in a society that had already undergone much reform. By 1970, over a decade after the first steps toward reform had been taken, Chile had seen far more change than Brazil ever had when Goulart became president. Congress had already passed the necessary legislation for agrarian reform, and Frei's administration (1964–70) had made significant progress in expropriating and redistributing unproductive large landholdings.[2] Frei had also done much to "Chileanize" copper and other foreign corporations, and Allende was to find little resistance in Congress when he submitted legislation to nationalize the large U.S. copper companies.[3]

Thus, when Allende was elected president in 1970, there was much room in Chile for a continuation of the changes initiated a decade earlier. With the exception of a minority of right-wingers, all political forces in Chilean society were in favor of at least a moderate extension of reforms.[4] Nevertheless, Allende's attempt to implement reforms led to one of the worst political conflicts in Chilean history. In the course of 1972, the Chilean polity became the site of a violent radicalization that in 1973 led to Allende's death and to the inauguration of one of the most authoritarian military regimes in Latin America. It is the task of this chapter to show that a prisoner's dilemma involving Chilean moderates, as explained in chapter 5, was at the root of the political conflict that led to the collapse of Chilean democracy.

Introduction to the Chilean Case

Chilean democracy had been one of the oldest and most stable Latin American democracies before it collapsed during Allende's term in September of 1973.[5] The most prominent member of the Socialist party and the candidate of the coalition of leftist parties called Popular Unity (UP—Unidad Popular), Salvador Allende had won the 1970 presidential elections by a margin of 39,000 votes out of three million total votes cast.[6] Allende obtained 36.2 percent of the votes, while Jorge Alessandri, the candidate of the right, obtained 34.9 percent, and Radomiro Tomic, from the centrist Christian Democratic Party (PDC), secured 27.8 percent of the votes.

Although Allende had received the highest plurality, his accession to the presidency was not automatic. The Chilean Constitution required that one of the candidates obtain more than half of the valid votes; otherwise, a joint session of both houses of Congress was to choose between the two candidates who had the highest plurality.[7] Thus, Allende's rise to the presidency depended on the joint approval of both houses of Congress. In effect, this meant that Allende's accession was contingent upon the support of the Christian Democrats, because his coalition was eighteen seats short of a majority in Congress, and the necessary additional votes could only come from the centrist PDC.[8] Traditionally, Congress had chosen the candidate with the highest plurality. But this was a very different case. Allende was a committed socialist and, although he had vowed to respect democratic procedures, he was distrusted by many Christian Democrats.

Just as a civilian-military coalition of right-wingers had attempted to stop Goulart's accession to the presidency in Brazil, an equivalent group tried to prevent Allende from assuming the chief executive office. Backed by U.S. corporations and the U.S. government, the Chilean right mounted a two-pronged attack against Allende and the Popular Unity.[9] On the one hand, efforts were made to induce Christian Democrats to vote against Allende in Congress. On the other hand, the conspirators tried to persuade military leaders to stage a coup.

But all attempts to prevent Allende's accession backfired. Christian Democratic congressmen could not be bribed, and Frei refused to participate in any scheme with the extreme right.[10] Furthermore, the PDC candidate, Radomiro Tomic, publicly supported Allende and urged congressmen of his party to vote for him.[11] As to the attempt to stage a coup, the commander-in-chief of the army, René Schneider, who was also a pro-American general, took a strong stance against the conspirators.[12] In reaction, the conspirators tried to abduct the general under the mistaken assumption that his kidnapping would instigate a coup. The plot backfired when the general resisted and his abductors shot him to death.

Although the PDC refused to participate in any conspiracy against Allende, many Christian Democrats were still reluctant to vote for him in the joint session of Congress.[13] After much debate within the PDC, the more conservative faction of the party agreed to vote for Allende on the condition that he support a constitutional amendment that would bind him to respect the civil liberties and freedoms prescribed by the democratic Chilean Constitution. When Allende and the Popular Unity agreed to pass what became the Statute of Democratic Guarantees (Estatuto de Guarantia), he was elected president by a majority of Congress on October 24, 1970.[14]

Not unlike Goulart's term, then, Allende's began on an ominous note. The Statute of Guarantees was clear evidence that the Christian Democratic Party, the largest party in the opposition, was hesitant to lend its support to Allende. Though the PDC was clearly committed to reforms, and its goals had much in common with Allende's, Christian Democrats were reluctant to back the Popular Unity government because they feared that it would transform Chile into another Cuba.[15] At the same time, Christian Democrats kept their distance from the right, and were unwilling to appeal to the military, but they were prepared to change their position in case the extremists in Allende's coalition were to gain the upper hand and Allende were tempted to violate the Statute of Guarantees.

The Possibility of Extending and Deepening the Reforms

Between 1965 and 1970 (the year Allende was elected), Frei's Christian Democratic government had passed new strong legislation that removed most obstacles to agrarian reform. This legislation enabled the Frei administration to expropriate more than 1,000 rural properties, totaling about 2,500,000 hectares, and to settle 20,000 families on the expropriated land.[16] In addition, Frei's government legalized peasant unionization, extended the minimum wage to the countryside, and helped create a variety of other organizations to mobilize and protect the interests of the population: 100,000 small landholders joined cooperatives, and 600,000 shantytown dwellers were helped in forming their own associations.[17] Government agencies also built more than 300,000 houses and greatly expanded primary education.[18]

The Frei government also broadened and strengthened the role of the state in promoting economic development. State ownership increased, especially in copper, steel, and electricity.[19] The Christian Democrats also had planned to continue expanding the control of the state over both the financial and industrial sectors of the economy, and to fully nationalize key foreign industries, such as the copper companies.

At the time of Allende's inauguration, then, previous administrations had already opened the road to a restructuring of Chilean society. Except for a minority at the right, most of the key Chilean political actors supported a continuation of the process of reform.[20] The disagreements were a matter of how quickly and how far that process should go. From Allende's perspective, the extension of reforms and the implementation of new ones were contingent upon the support of the Christian Democrats. Allende's coalition, the Popular Unity, controlled only 40 percent of the seats in each of the houses, while the PDC had 35 percent in the Chamber of Deputies and 44 percent in the Senate. If Allende was to use democratic means to transform Chile into a socialist society, he needed the cooperation of the Christian Democrats.

Cooperation between Allende and the PDC was perfectly possible. In the context of Chile in the early seventies, both Allende and the Christian Democrats were moderates. It may seem inappropriate to call Allende a moderate leftist and the Christian

Democrats moderate rightists. Obviously, compared to their Brazilian counterparts, Allende was further to the left then Goulart; and the PDC was also clearly further to the left than the PSD. But in the course of the sixties the whole Chilean political system shifted to the left. Compared to Allende, then, the Christian Democrats were moderate rightists. And, relative to the extremists in the Popular Unity coalition, Allende was clearly a moderate leftist.

As a matter of fact, Allende was the most moderate political force within his coalition.[21] A true idealist, Allende genuinely believed he could bring socialism to Chile strictly by democratic means. Ironically, Allende had more support among the communists than among his own Socialist party. Of the two largest parties of the Popular Unity, the Communist was the more moderate party.[22] Though ultimately less committed to representative democracy than Allende, the Communist party advocated a more cautious and gradual approach to change than did the Socialist party. It also backed Allende in his efforts to reach a compromise with the Christian Democrats, and repeatedly urged the extremists of the left to refrain from using radical tactics.

Allende's own party, however, was badly split. The right wing of the Socialist party was supportive of Allende, but the left wing was strongly in favor of arming the population to smash the capitalist system. The radical socialists supported the extremist MIR (Movimiento de Izquierda Revolucionário), whose members believed that only a violent popular uprising could give birth to a socialist society.[23]

Allende's coalition, the Popular Unity, was thus divided in two. If we include the small parties, Allende's moderate left consisted of the communists, the left wing of the Radical Party, the moderate socialists, and part of the MAPU (Movimiento de Acción Popular Unitario—formed by the most leftist members of the PDC).[24] On the other hand, the extreme left consisted of the radical faction of the Socialist party, the extremists of the MAPU, and the MIR.

Both Allende and the Christian Democrats shared a strong commitment to representative democracy. Like Allende and the moderate left, Christian Democrats also wanted Chile to break out of its dependence on imperialist nations and to develop along noncapitalist lines. Nevertheless, they were equally critical of

Marxism, wishing that Chile would follow a third "communitarian" road—though Christian Democrats were vague as to what this might mean.[25] Even the most leftist Christian Democrats did not want the state to have total ownership and control of the economy. Their ideal was much closer to social democracy—a mixed economy with a great deal of worker participation and a large welfare apparatus—than to Allende's democratic socialism.

The moderate politicians of the PDC were also divided. Whereas more conservative Christian Democrats distrusted Allende and wished to keep open the possibility of an alliance with the extremist right-wingers of the National Party, the leftist wing of the party led by Tomic wanted the PDC to align itself behind Allende and the moderate left.[26] As a result, major leaders of the PDC made it clear that the party would give only conditional support to Allende. If Allende extended the reforms through normal constitutional channels—that is, in consultation with Congress—all would be well. If, on the other hand, the extremists gained the upper hand, and Allende failed to control them, the PDC would withdraw its support. This was no idle threat. Such a withdrawal was likely to stimulate a radicalization of the moderates of both the left and the right, with obvious negative consequences for Chilean democracy.

The Moderates' Dilemma

Initially, Allende was not as dependent as Goulart had been on the approval of Congress to implement his reforms. The essential legislation to expropriate and redistribute land had been passed. And, as we shall see, Allende could rely on a series of past legal provisions to expand state ownership and control of the economy. This did not mean, however, that Allende and the Popular Unity could do as they pleased. That Allende, in the short run, could extend the reforms with little support from the PDC in Congress did not mean that the Christian Democrats were defenseless. They could always pass new legislation to control both the extent and the pace of change, thus setting constitutional limits to what Allende and the Popular Unity could do, for together, the Christian Democrats and the extreme right held 60 percent of the seats in both houses of Congress.[27]

Thus, although the extension of reforms in Chile was not contingent upon a formal agreement between the moderates of the left and the right, it did nevertheless rest on the implicit understanding that Allende and the Popular Unity would eventually negotiate with the Christian Democrats an agreement concerning the future relationship between the state and the Chilean economy. The leadership of the PDC assumed that Allende would try to reach a compromise with his opposition. Otherwise, he would find it almost impossible, as he eventually did, to achieve his goals within a democratic framework.

In the end, Allende and the Christian Democrats failed to reach an agreement either on the limits of state ownership of the economy or on the pace and methods by which the state should take over private corporations. Although both moderate sides would have preferred reaching an agreement to an all-out confrontation, each side feared that the other was using the extremists in its own camp to impose its will on the other. The moderates of the PDC feared that Allende was playing a double-faced game, waiting for the right moment to seize power and to establish a socialist dictatorship. On the other hand, Allende and the moderates of the Popular Unity feared that the Christian Democrats would ultimately join the extremists of the right in ousting Allende from power.

To reassure each other, the moderates would thus have to break with their extremist allies (or potential allies) unequivocally. Unfortunately, as we shall now see, each side stood to gain more from keeping its radical allies no matter what the other side did. Just like the Brazilian moderates, the Chileans were caught in a prisoner's dilemma game in which the rational strategy for each side was to maintain its ties to the extremists in its own coalition.

Mutual Fears

The political strategy Allende pursued during his first year only exacerbated the fears of the Christian Democrats. Knowing that to seek the approval of Christian Democratic congressmen would only slow down the construction of a socialist economy, Allende used a stratagem that enabled him legally to eschew the consent of Congress. To expropriate major banks and key industries rapidly, Allende relied on pieces of legislation passed in

1932, 1955, and 1966, which allowed the government to intervene in and expropriate firms which either "unjustifiedly" failed to produce essential goods and services for the population or were paralyzed by labor disputes.[28] Using this legislation, the Popular Unity could easily seize banks and industries it wanted to control. Firms could be requisitioned or expropriated on the allegation that they were deficient in their production of goods and services of "primary necessity." Failing this, workers could always open the way to intervention by forcing plants to halt their operations. In addition, the government could force a corporation into bankruptcy by raising wages and keeping prices down, thereby allowing authorities to purchase its shares at considerably lower cost.

Allende's use of these methods to nationalize major portions of the private sector of the economy eventually was to trigger the conflict between the Popular Unity and the Christian Democrats that brought down the democratic regime. But at the start of Allende's term, the leadership of the Popular Unity felt it could neutralize the opposition. Although the leaders of Popular Unity were aware of the possibility that their nationalization policy could lead to a major decrease in private investment and provoke strong opposition from the PDC and the right, they believed they had a good chance to both offset disinvestment and neutralize the opposition.

Pedro Vuskovic, Allende's minister of the economy, devised a plan deliberately designed to offset private disinvestment and to counter opposition from the PDC.[29] The plan's ultimate objective was to achieve in the short run a massive redistribution of income with a simultaneous rise in the rate of economic growth. A rapid and extensive increase of the incomes of wage and salary earners would stimulate demand and economic growth. As the economic situation improved, and the middle and lower classes benefited from nationalization, redistribution, and growth, popular support for the Popular Unity would grow. Such a swelling of support could then be used to pressure the Christian Democrats to join Allende in transforming Chile into a socialist society.

The Vuskovic plan was based on two assumptions. First, it was assumed that the transfer of private enterprises to the public sector would enable the government to invest more extensively and effectively in the economic development of the country. According to government leaders, the nationalization of private enterprises would stop the escape of massive profits to foreign banks. By investing these formerly lost funds in the development of the country, an enlarged public sector would more than offset the losses in private investment resulting from the nationalization policy of the Popular Unity government. In addition, government officials also believed that the new surpluses generated by nationalization would also compensate for the planned increase in public spending that would be necessary to expand social services for the lower classes.

The second assumption underlying the Vuskovic plan was that the Chilean economy was operating at a sufficiently high degree of idle capacity to absorb the massive increase in demand that would result from the government's effort to increase the wages and salaries of the middle and lower classes. The policymakers of Allende's government reasoned that the excess capacity would be sufficient to arrest the inflationary pressure that might otherwise result from their decision to increase wages while simultaneously keeping down the prices of basic commodities. Thus, the government's policymakers thought they could have the best of all worlds—nationalization and redistribution with economic growth and without either inflation or a drainage of foreign reserves. Should such a miraculous performance occur, of course, Popular Unity would mobilize so much popular support as to neutralize any opposition from the right.

But the Vuskovic plan did not work as intended. During the first year of his administration, Allende engaged in a massive effort to expand the state's economic power, to extend the agrarian reform, and to redistribute income. By the end of 1971, the government had seized or was in the process of seizing seventy major industrial establishments and had fully nationalized foreign copper corporations.[30] The government had also nationalized twenty-six private banks, two of which were U.S.-owned, which allowed it to control most of the credit flow in Chile.[31] As for the agrarian reform, Allende and the Popular Unity coalition expropriated over 1,300 properties during 1971 alone, a number which exceeded the total property seizures of six years of the previous administration.[32] In addition, the government raised the basic wage by almost 67 percent over the previous year, and by the middle of 1971 the average income per employee had increased by 55 percent.[33] All of these actions were accompanied by a great expansion of social services such as education, health, housing, and sanitation.

Although at first the sharp increase in demand generated by the government's spending and its redistributive measures stimulated economic growth, by the end of 1971 the inflated demand could no longer be met. By then, the level of demand had clearly exceeded the country's production and import capacities. The Vuskovic plan had clearly overestimated the idle capacity of the Chilean economy. In addition, the enlarged public sector failed to generate the increase in revenues necessary to offset the losses due to the drastic decrease in private investment, and the sharp cutbacks in foreign aid and credit, following the takeover of private firms.[34] Beset by continual demands for higher wages and by strikes, work stoppages, bloated employment rolls, managerial inefficiency, and strict price controls, state enterprises lost large sums of money in 1972 and 1973.[35]

As demand lagged behind production and the government could no longer control prices without producing enormous shortages, prices soared. Inflation rose from 22 percent in 1971 to 46 percent in July of 1972, reaching 163 percent by December.[36] The need to import, as well as a drop in the price of copper, drained foreign reserves, which fell from $343 million to $32 million in the course of 1971.[37] By the end of the following year, Chile would have a net deficit in reserves of $289 million. The situation was further aggravated by budget deficits. To continue investing in development, cover the losses of state enterprises, maintain its ambitious redistributive programs, and finance the agrarian reform, the government had to cover an ever larger part of its budget with new money emissions. By 1972, the proportion of the budget covered by emissions had increased by at least 30 percent over the previous year.[38]

By the end of 1971, the deterioration of the economic situation had triggered considerable protest. Far from widening the government's base of support, the economic program adopted by Allende increased popular discontent. Instead of making middle-class converts to the Popular Unity's cause, the government's economic policies intensified the opposition from that class. In December, five thousand women staged the famous "March of the Empty Pots" in protest against the inflationary measures of the

Allende administration.[39] Even among its own working-class constituents, the Popular Unity government met with more and more discontent. Between 1970 and 1972, the number of strikes increased by 170 percent; the substantial redistribution of income promoted by Allende only stimulated an ever greater popular demand for more material benefits.[40]

Needless to say, all of these events did not encourage the moderates of the right, the Christian Democrats, to align themselves with Allende. On the contrary, Allende's actions during his first year in office greatly reinforced their fears. The government's use of obscure pieces of legislation and of rather underhanded methods to seize and expropriate private banks and firms accentuated the Christian Democrats' distrust of Allende and the Popular Unity, pushing them further toward the right-wingers of the National Party.[41] Their suspicions of Allende seemed to be further confirmed by the violent activities of the extremists in the Popular Unity.[42] The MIR and other radical groups often supplied organizational support and weapons to rural workers, provoking a veritable explosion in land seizures during the first year of Allende's government. The radicals also engaged in various urban forms of revolutionary tactics, ranging from bank robbery to political assassination.

Allende and the moderates within the Popular Unity, especially the communists, were strongly opposed to the radicals' methods.[43] But they did nothing beyond admonishing the extremists in their camp. Naturally, Allende's failure to stop the radicals compounded the trepidations harbored by the Christian Democrats that he was playing a double game—waiting for the opportunity to install a revolutionary government. It mattered little that much of the violence perpetrated by the left was a response to similar actions by the extreme right; the moderates of the right blamed the leniency of the government toward the radicals for the mounting political violence that followed Allende's rise to power.

In spite of repeated demands by the Christian Democrats that Allende take harsher measures against the radicals within his coalition, he refused to exclude or to repress them.[44] Quite aside from their ideological respect for the radical socialists and for groups like the MIR, Allende and the moderates of the left had strong instrumental reasons for maintaining their alliance with the extremists. They had good reason to fear the Christian Democrats, who were showing a willingness to form alliances with the extremists within their own camp. In the first two months of 1972, the PDC cooperated with the parties of the extreme right in two important by-elections, it joined those parties in impeaching the minister of the interior, and it threatened to support the National Party's proposal to impeach the minister of the economy.[45]

The Defection of the Moderates

As the end of 1971 neared it became apparent that Allende's and the Popular Unity's strategy to force the Christian Democrats into compliance would not work. By later October, the Christian Democrats had hardened their position toward the government. After publicly accusing Allende of playing a two-faced game, the leadership of the PDC began to consider an alliance with the extreme right.[46] Together, the PDC and the extremists of the right had the majority in Congress that could end the government's use of underhanded methods to seize and expropriate enterprises in the private sector of the economy. At this point it became clear that only an agreement between Allende and the Christian Democrats on the limits and criteria of expropriation could arrest the radicalization and eventual collapse of Chilean democracy.

Among the government's economic plans, the one that did the most to prompt the Christian Democrats' retaliatory actions was the Popular Unity's intended takeover of the country's only private paper industry, the Paper and Carton Manufacturing Company, headed by Jorge Alessandri, one of the most prominent leaders of the right.[47] The Christian Democrats and the extreme right feared that Allende's takeover of Alessandri's paper company would subject the national press to the control of Popular Unity. As the government attempted to bankrupt the private paper company, the right defended the company by establishing the National Freedom Fund to buy shares from any of the company's stockholders who wanted to sell. In addition, the National Party proposed that Congress impeach Allende's minister of the economy in order to regain some control over the government's expansion of the economic power of the state.[48]

To prevent the PDC from voting to impeach his minister, Allende agreed to submit to Congress legislation regulating the nationalization of the economy. Late in October, the president sent a bill to Congress which proposed to divide the economy into three sectors—social (state-owned), mixed, and private.[49] Although the bill limited expropriations to firms that had assets totaling more than $1 million as of the end of 1969, it was far from meeting the demands of both the moderates and the extremists of the right.

As a counterproposal, the Christian Democrats presented a constitutional amendment which retained the division of the economy into the three areas proposed by the government's bill.[50] It also accepted the bill's provisions to place under state control the fields of mining, transportation, communication, gas, petroleum, cement, steel, nitrate, iodine, and arms production. But the constitutional amendment severely curtailed Allende's capacity to create a socialist economy. The amendment transferred to the legislature the ultimate power to move industries from the private sector to the state or mixed areas of the economy. The seizure or expropriation of industries could be carried out only by specific congressional legislation.

The proposed constitutional amendment on the division of the economy marked a dramatic shift in the Christian Democratic attitude toward the Popular Unity government. It indicated clearly that the Christian Democrats were now more determined than ever to put stringent limits on Allende's efforts to place the economy under the ownership and control of the state. Taking advantage of the growing discontent stemming from the deteriorating economic situation, the PDC submitted its constitutional amendment to a vote in Congress in February 1972.[51] The full Congress met and the majority opposition passed the amendment. As provided in the Constitution, it was then sent to the president for his corrections and modifications.

The passage of the amendment regulating the economy led to a political crisis that was to be fatal to Chilean democracy. Each of the moderate sides—Allende and the Christian Democrats—sought to defeat the other by trying to use to its advantage deficiencies and omissions in the text of the constitutional reforms that had been passed under the Frei administration.[52] Adopted in 1970, these reforms did not specify the type of vote necessary for the Congress to override a presidential veto of a constitutional amendment. Since the Christian Democrats and the extreme right had a simple majority in Congress, they claimed that such a majority was sufficient to override a veto. If the president disagreed, they argued, the constitutional reforms entitled him to call a plebiscite to decide on the matter. Allende, on the other hand, fearing that he would not win such a plebiscite, claimed that Congress needed a two-thirds vote to override his veto of the constitutional amendment. Should Congress disagree, he would submit the matter to the new Constitutional Tribunal, where Allende felt he could obtain a favorable decision. To this the Christian Democrats responded that the tribunal was not authorized to interpret amendments to the Constitution.

The impasse created by the constitutional amendment promised to end in a violent confrontation unless the moderates reached an agreement on limits to the economy's nationalization. Given that no authority that could make a final decision on the constitutional issue was acceptable to both sides, the only solution to the crisis was an agreement on the *substance* of the amendment regulating the expansion of the state's economic power. But the moderates could only reach an agreement if each side repudiated its own extremist allies.[53] The Christian Democrats were not about to make major concessions on the nationalization of the economy unless Allende could reassure them that he would no longer allow the radicals in the Popular Unity coalition to use semilegal and illegal means toward a rapid construction of a socialist society. And Allende would not agree to impose significant limits to, and reduce the pace of, the expansion of the state's control over the economy unless the Christian Democrats reassured him that they would not join the extreme right to prevent the Popular Unity government from achieving at least a significant expansion of the state's economic power.

But neither Allende nor the Christian Democrats could break with the extremists in their respective camps. They both knew that if either one of them irreversibly repudiated the extremists, the other would have a major advantage in *not* doing the same. Like Goulart before him, Allende knew that if he took harsh measures to control the radicals within his coalition he would sow discord among the ranks of the Popular Unity, which would make him and his whole socialist project extremely vulnerable to attack by a coalition of the Christian Democrats and the extreme right. Allende knew that if he and the moderates of the Popular Unity turned against the radicals, the Christian Democrats would have a strong incentive to maintain their own ties to the extreme right. By the same token, the Christian Democrats also felt that they could not cut their ties to the right-wingers of the National Party. For if they did, they would lose their power to stop Allende and the Popular Unity from seizing power and imposing a socialist society in Chile. If the Christian Democrats were to break relations with the extremist right-wingers, it would be to the advantage of the moderates of the Popular Unity not to break with their radical allies.

Unable to turn against their extremist allies, the moderates of the Popular Unity and the Christian Democrats would never meet halfway on the issue of state control. Rather than finding a way out of the impasse, they were led by the prisoner's dilemma in which they were entangled to wait for a decisive confrontation at the polls—the congressional elections of 1973.[54] Both moderate parties felt they could then win the decisive majority that would free them from having to compromise their goals. But their refusal to compromise in the course of 1972 gave the extremists a chance to radicalize the situation and to drive the moderates further and further apart. By the time the congressional elections of 1973 took place it was too late to prevent the breakdown of democratic institutions in Chile.

The Failure to Reach an Agreement

Between March and July of 1972, Allende and the Christian Democrats tried twice to resolve the impasse over the constitutional amendment. Since neither side was really willing to break with the extremists, both attempts failed to yield an agreement on the critical issues concerning the expansion of state control over the economy.

The first round of talks took place in March.[55] Representing Allende, the PIR (Partido de Izquierda Radical) entered into extensive negotiations with the Christian Democrats. Although Manuel Sanhueza, the PIR minister of justice, claimed that the talks had led to an agreement on the regulation of government takeovers of private firms, Allende sent to Congress on April 6 a counterproposal that clearly deviated from the Sanhueza agreement. He did so because the radicals in his coalition had rejected Sanhueza's agreement.[56] In addition, backed by the socialists, Pedro Vuskovic, Allende's minister of the economy, boycotted the talks by carrying out a series of expropriations of doubtful legality.[57] These expropriations prompted the PIR to leave Popular Unity and join the opposition, further isolating Allende and forcing him to move even closer to the radical socialists.

After the first round of negotiations broke down and the conflict over the amendment moved into the streets, Allende and the moderates of Popular Unity made another attempt to reach a compromise with the opposition. Initially conducted in secret, the second round of negotiations occurred in June 1972.[58] Jorge Tapia, Allende's new minister of justice, and Senator Renan Fuentealba, the president of the PDC, succeeded in settling the most fundamental issues between the two moderate sides. Both sides made substantial concessions, and while the resulting agreement gave significant power to Congress over the expropriation of private firms, it still left Allende with considerable discretion over state control of the country's most strategic industries.

Although both Allende and the Christian Democratic leadership supported the Tapia-Fuentealba agreement, the conservative wing of the PDC and the extremists of the right strongly opposed it. Unwilling to sever their ties with these right wingers, the moderate leadership of the PDC joined them in breaking off the negotiations only two weeks after they had begun. When the deadline for a Senate vote on Allende's counterproposals arrived, the conservative Christian Democrats forced a negative vote that ended all possibilities of reaching an agreement on the constitutional amendment concerning the state's control over the economy. By then, the Christian Democrats were convinced that Allende and the Popular Unity government "could be dealt with only from a position of unquestioned strength."[59] The same was true of the radicals in Allende's coalition, who were pleased with the decision of the Christian Democrats to break off the Tapia-Fuentealba negotiations.

Confrontation and Collapse

From July 1972, when negotiations between Allende and the PDC failed, to September 1973, when the military ousted Allende and the Popular Unity government, the Chilean political system became increasingly divided into two warring camps. The moderates of the right and the left grew further and further apart, playing into the hands of the extremists who wanted to seize power by force. When the congressional elections failed to resolve the constitutional issue and to break the stalemate between the left and the right, Allende was forced to rely on the only institution left that was considered to be relatively neutral and could therefore serve as arbiter—the Chilean military.[60]

But as soon as the military was drawn into the political arena it was engulfed in the conflict between the civilians. Instead of arbitrating the conflict, the military was itself politicized and divided by it.[61] The double threat of socialism and the undoing of military institutions finally led the legalist Chilean officers to join the conspirators of the right in staging the coup that ousted the government in September of 1973.

Radicalization

The moderates' failure to reach an agreement gave the extremists an opportunity to escalate the conflict and to force a confrontation between the left and the right. Short of a violent confrontation, the congressional elections scheduled for March 1973 offered the only way out of the impasse created by the passage of the constitutional amendment. If either Allende or the Christian Democrats won a majority of the seats in Congress, the winner could then impose its own program through democratic channels. To this end both Allende and the PDC made a massive effort to mobilize voters during the second half of 1972.[62] Each side tried to outdo the other in organizing public demonstrations—as proof of the popular support it could muster. This gave the extremists free rein in promoting a wave of confrontations which created an atmosphere of impending civil war for the remainder of Allende's term.

The extremists were also favored by the deteriorating economic situation, which led to the massive political involvement of the *gremios*—associations representing occupational and small business groups.[63] Frightened by the government's nationalization of the economy and by its rationing of supplies, the middle class went on strike. In late August, retail merchants declared a national one-day strike, and in October, truckers went on strike for an indefinite period of time. The trucking industry strike was joined by numerous other groups and almost paralyzed the economy. According to some estimates, nearly 100 percent of transport and commerce, 80 percent of the professions, and 85 percent of peasant cooperatives joined the strike.[64]

The strikes and demonstrations of businessmen and middle-class groups not only forced the moderate Christian Democrats further toward the extreme right but also led to a counteractive mobilization on the part of the left.[65] The government used the *Juntas de Abastecimientos y Precios* (Juntas for Supplies and Prices), which had been created to distribute food and goods to the poorer neighborhoods, to create a vast network for rationing supplies. With the help of the Central Labor Confederation (CUT), the government also organized students, workers, and professionals to participate in counterstrikes against the right. As for the radicals, they set up paramilitary units—*comandos comunales, comandos campesinos,* and *cordones industriales*—to protect communities, farms, and factories under the control of the left.

Toward the end of 1972, the situation had grown chaotic. Faced with mounting confrontation and violence, soaring inflation, and a nearly paralyzed economy, Allende had to bring the military into the government.[66] This move was necessary both to negotiate a settlement with the strikers and to restore confidence in the democratic process. The appointment as minister of interior of the army commander-in-chief, General Carlos Prats, was seen as necessary to the guarantee of fair and free congressional elections in March of 1973. Appointed on November 5, 1972, Prats did help to negotiate an end to the truckers' strike and to restore a measure of confidence in the democratic process. But the elections of March did little to resolve the fundamental conflict between Allende and the Christian Democrats.[67] Popular Unity failed to secure a majority of seats, nor did the right obtain the two-thirds majority in Congress that would have allowed it to override a presidential veto.

Even worse, the Prats appointment divided the military.[68] The more conservative among them felt that Prats was legitimizing the government and the left. To avoid a further politicization of the military and the impression that the more moderate officers were allowing the left to achieve its subversive goals, Prats resigned in March. Still trying to steer a middle course, Allende appointed a new cabinet composed of moderate members from Popular Unity. But the conflict continued to escalate, this time fueled by the government's school-reform plan to create a Unified National Schooling System (*Escuela Nacional Unificada,* ENU), which the opposition attacked as an attempt to turn the educational system into a massive indoctrination program.[69]

After both the church and the military condemned ENU, Allende was forced to withdraw the proposal. In retaliation, the Popular Unity cabinet moved to expropriate forty firms that had been occupied during the strikes of 1972.[70] These expropriations, in turn, led the Christian Democrats and the military to harden their positions. In May 1973, former president Frei persuaded the Christian Democrats that they were facing the threat of a Marxist dictatorship and that they had to take an unambiguous hard-line stance toward Allende and the Popular Unity.[71] The election of Senator Aylwin to the presidency of the PDC indicated that Frei's position had won. The conservatives were now in control of the PDC, which meant that the party would consider a political solution to the conflict only if Allende accepted unconditionally all of their demands.

In early June, the Constitutional Tribunal ruled that it was not competent to judge the constitutional issue, and the opposition moved to impeach four of Allende's ministers and eight of his provincial intendants.[72] By then, rightist politicians and the right-wing press were openly asking the military to intervene.[73] In response, the left organized a massive rally in support of the government. A week later, on June 29, 1973, a small military contingent attempted the first coup against the government.[74] The coup was easily put down by the legalist military under the leadership of Prats. Nevertheless, it showed that the cohesion of the military was severely threatened, which ultimately led the reluctant legalist military to intervene against the Popular Unity government.

The Collapse of Chilean Democracy

The attempted coup of June 29 hardened not only the military but also leftist radicals. It painfully brought to light the relative powerlessness of the radicals, who, realizing they could have done nothing to defend themselves, now openly called for the mass mobilization and arming of workers.[75] In spite of Allende's and the moderate left's vehement opposition to armed insurrection, the strident calls to action of the extremists were sufficient to trigger a concerted campaign of the armed forces against the left. Fearing that the left was forming a parallel army and instigating insubordination among the troops, the military invoked a law on arms control that allowed them to legally wage war on the left.[76] From July onward, the military routinely organized raids in search of weapons, broke into government factories and party headquarters, and arrested radical leaders. Rather than breaking its will, the crackdown further enhanced the left's determination to arm the workers and to incite enlisted men to rebel against their superiors.

It was in the midst of this renewed turmoil that Allende tried once more to reach an agreement with the Christian Democrats. With the help of moderate politicians respected by both sides, arrangements were made for a meeting between Allende and Aylwin, the president of the PDC.[77] The meeting was cordial, but it failed to produce an agreement. Among other things, the Christian Democrats demanded that Allende bring the military in at all levels of government as proof of his good faith. But Allende refused to govern under the tutelage of the military.

As it became clear a week later, however, Allende was only saving face by refusing to comply with Aylwin's demands. The decline of the economy, the growing political radicalization, and a new round of national strikes left him no choice but to reprimand the radicals and to turn to the military for help. Thus, in early August Allende accepted all of the conditions required by the armed forces to form a "national security" cabinet.[78] For the first time, Allende took a strong stand against the radicals in his coalition. As he inaugurated his "national security" cabinet—drawn from the legalist military, including General Prats himself—Allende harshly and openly criticized the revolutionary left for infiltrating the military and for their other radical activities.[79] But it was too late. Even the moderate legalist officers could not stop the downfall of the regime.

The Christian Democrats were now convinced that Allende had to be deposed: they openly supported the strikers and tacitly supported military intervention.[80] On August 22 the Chamber of Deputies adopted a resolution stating that the government was unconstitutional, and General Prats was pressured into resigning both as minister of defense and as army commander. Although at first his successor, General Augusto Pinochet, assured the government that the army would remain neutral, it did not take him long to change his mind. Less than three weeks after Prats's resignation, on September 11, 1973, Allende lost his life defending his government against the military coup.

8 CONCLUSION

Explanations of the breakdown of democratic regimes tend to attribute it to structural causes. They see tensions, contradictions, and crises in economic, political, and social structures as determining the collapse of democratic institutions. This structural mode of explanation tends to be deterministic, to see the breakdown of democracy as inevitable, and to view the main actors involved as helpless in the face of sweeping structural change.

According to this perspective, structural forces compel human beings, often unwittingly, to act in ways that promote the development of those forces. In this sense, the intentions and goals of actors are irrelevant to explain phenomena like the collapse of democracy. Whatever their intentions, structural forces propel them to act so as to bring about the breakdown necessary to the alleviation of structural tensions or to the resolution of structural contradictions. When these tensions and contradictions require them to, the actors involved will act and interact in prescribed ways so as to usher in the authoritarian regime that will either save capitalist institutions, or promote economic development, or move the political system out of decisional paralysis, or achieve any of the other purposes history in its infinite cunning wants achieved.

In this book, I have offered a radically different view and explanation of the collapse of democratic institutions. In my explanation, structural conditions do not determine the behavior of actors and the subsequent breakdown of democracy. Structures are seen as sets of constraints and opportunities that narrow the possible courses of action in a given situation but always leave available more than one alternative to the actors involved. Although the actors face difficult economic and political structural problems, they in principle have the choice to act in ways that can prevent the breakdown of democratic institutions. This breakdown is therefore far from inevitable. It is largely contingent upon the beliefs, preferences, and goals of the actors involved. According to this view and mode of explanation—which I have labeled "intentional"—although constrained by the past and the structural arrangements under which they live, human beings also make history.

As my analysis of the Latin American cases has shown, structural tensions did not preclude the preservation of democratic institutions. The main actors involved could have chosen courses of action that would have prevented the collapse of democracy and the emergence of authoritarianism. Had the actors ranked the preservation of democratic institutions far above any other goal, they might have avoided the rise of dictatorship. Unfortunately, the attempts of the left to push reforms to a maximum level, on the one hand, and those of the right to keep them at a minimum, on the other, threw them into a prisoner's dilemma situation that ultimately led to the breakdown of the democratic regime and the rise of a military dictatorship nobody really wanted. The actors had to choose within difficult structural constraints, of course, but in the end it was their own preferences that led them to choose courses of action that had disastrous consequences for the democratic process.

From a methodological point of view, these conclusions have important implications for the nature of explanation in the social sciences. Against the determinism of structural explanations, the analysis carried out in this book confirms the conjecture that one cannot explain events, structures, or change on the basis of a set of initial structural conditions alone. Economic, state, and class structures can only broadly define the set of feasible alternatives for actors in a particular situation at a given point in time. They cannot explain the actors' behavior, nor the outcomes resulting from their strategic interaction. To explain their behavior and interaction, as well as the outcomes that result, one needs to know the actors' goals, preferences, and beliefs—and how the actors mutually condition one another's choices.

My examination of the literature on the breakdown of democratic regimes in Latin America has shown that the most prominent structural explanations of these phenomena are fundamentally flawed. I have shown that structuralists fail to explain this collapse because they use invalid explanatory strategies which they mistakenly believe to be appropriate. Structuralists have claimed that one can successfully explain historical outcomes like the collapse of democratic institutions by direct reference to structural conditions, without any mention of human beliefs, preferences, and intentions. As I have shown extensively in chapter 3, however, structural explanations can only dismiss intentional phenomena by resorting either to functional arguments or to unexamined assumptions about the causal links between structural conditions and the interests and values of the actors involved.

Whether they resort to functionalism or to assumptions about the interests of actors, structural explanations of the breakdown of democratic regimes prove to be deficient. My scrutiny of these explanations revealed that most of them employ a functional argument: the collapse of democracy and the rise of dictatorship are explained by a need to "solve" structural problems. It is usually argued that when democratic institutions can no longer perform functions necessary to the survival of economic or political structures, these institutions will give way to more authoritarian forms of government. The collapse of democracy and the emergence of dictatorship are explained by the latter's function in maintaining severely threatened societal structures. Authoritarianism is explained, for example, as necessary to the survival of capitalist institutions in the throes of a severe crisis, or as essential to suppress conflicts that a polarized party system can no longer manage, or even as indispensable to revive a political system suffering from "decisional paralysis."

As I showed in chapters 2 and 3, none of these structural and functional explanations tells us exactly how endangered politico-economic arrangements substitute the authoritarian regime that will guarantee their survival for the democratic institutions that no longer can do so. In other words, structural explanations of democratic breakdowns that resort to functional arguments do not spell out the causal mechanism linking structural crisis to those breakdowns and to the emergence of dictatorial regimes. Yet spelling out the causal mechanism is a requisite of a successful functional explanation. Otherwise, one cannot be sure that the phenomenon being explained was caused by its function. The fact that an authoritarian regime may actually have beneficial effects on a capitalist economy in crisis does not mean that these effects bring it about; the dictatorship might have been caused by something entirely different.

To show that the consequences (function) of the authoritarian regime caused its emergence, one has to spell out how exactly the structures which benefit from these consequences engender such a regime. And the structural/functional explanations of the collapse of democracy in Latin America have so far failed to provide such a causal mechanism. Conceivably, structuralists might sometime in the future successfully specify the causal link necessary to justify their functionalist arguments. I do not think this will happen. As I have discussed at length in the early chapters of this book, in functional explanations the actors who bring about the beneficial consequences are unaware of these effects and bring them about only unintentionally. Yet in all cases of the emergence of authoritarianism, at least some of the actors who bring it about are fully aware of its consequences and do so intentionally.

Structuralists that do not use functional arguments do not fare much better. In their attempts to construct a direct causal link between structures and outcomes and to avoid any reference to human intentions, structuralists implicitly assume that societal arrangements determine the values and interests of the human beings who live under them. The most common example of this type of assumption is the one by which one's position in the class structure would determine one's interests, which in turn would determine one's behavior. If this were the case, one could explain and predict many outcomes directly from knowledge of the characteristics of class structures. Knowledge about the preferences and intentions of individuals would be unnecessary and redundant, for it could be inferred from information about the class structure of the society to which they belonged.

As I have shown in the first part of the book, however, these nonfunctionalist structural explanations fail to provide satisfactory explanations of the breakdown of democracy (and of social revolutions). Structuralists have been unable to make correct inferences about the beliefs, interests, preferences, and intentions of actors solely from the structural arrangements under which these actors live. As I have shown in my analysis of the breakdown of democracy, for example, actors belonging to the same class had widely different ideas about what their interests were and how they should act during the crisis situations preceding the collapse of democratic regimes. It was precisely this variety of preferences and goals among members of the same class, and among those claiming to represent the same class, that led to the conflicts resulting in the breakdown of democratic institutions. Without knowledge of the specific goals and preferences of the actors involved—a knowledge that structuralists have not been able to infer from the features of societal structures—it is therefore impossible to provide an adequate explanation of the collapse of democracy.

It may well be that in the future, nonfunctionalist structuralists will be more successful in specifying direct causal links between structures and the outcomes they are supposed to explain. I suspect they never will. In most situations human beings have a choice. To the extent that this is the case, explanations of human behavior and its outcomes must specify the causal mechanisms underlying human choices. To forge the causal links between structure and behavior, structuralists must therefore explain not only how structural arrangements constrain behavior—which they successfully do—but also how actors choose among the alternative courses of action those arrangements permit.

My defense of a form of explanation that includes the beliefs, preferences, goals, and calculations of actors—of intentional explanation—in no way implies that structural conditions are of no relevance. The position I have taken in this book speaks for structures as having a reality of their own, which cannot be simplistically reduced to the actions of individuals. My view of structural conditions as a set of constraints and opportunities defining the feasible alternatives for actors involved in a given situation precludes both the reductionism of individualists, who see structures as nothing but collections of individual actions, and the naïveté of the voluntarists, who fail to acknowledge the structural constraints under which individuals act.

It was with the purpose of avoiding the pitfalls of both structuralist and individualist/voluntarist explanations that I presented in this book an intentional explanation of the breakdown of democratic regimes. Like all intentional explanatory approaches, my explanation includes both structural conditions and the intentions of the actors involved in the breakdown. I showed how, given their structurally defined alternatives and their preferences, the actors took into account each other's possible choices to decide on a strategy of action. Using rational-choice theory and game theory, I showed that the actors were in a prisoner's dilemma situation which prevented cooperation and led to the collapse of democratic institutions.

Needless to say, far more work has to be done to determine whether or not my explanation applies to a wider range of cases. It remains to be seen whether my explanation applies to the other Latin American cases of breakdown of democracy and to some of the prewar European cases, such as the collapse of the Weimar Republic or the emergence of fascism in Italy. As I suggested in chapter 5, in all of these cases the collapse of democracy followed a process of radicalization of the left and the right that moderate forces were unable to contain. There is thus good reason to presume that the model I proposed applies to these cases as well.

It is possible, of course, that further research might show that other cases might best be modeled by games other than the prisoner's dilemma. But whatever the shortcomings of my particular explanation, I hope that I have at least made a good case for the use of intentional explanations in the study of large-scale political transformations, such as the collapse of democracy and the rise of authoritarianism, revolutions, war, and like phenomena.

I would also like to think that this book will help in restoring confidence in our capacity to preserve democracy in the face of adversity. Although recent world events have not been unfavorable to the spread of democratic institutions, these are everywhere under pressure. Understandably, widespread poverty and acute inequalities promote an urgent desire for social reforms, an urgency which more often than not clashes with democratic processes. The severe tensions between reform and democracy may create the illusion that they are mutually exclusive. But this is not so. As my analysis suggests, implementing reforms within a democratic context may be a difficult balancing act, but it is possible. It can only be done, however, if reforms are implemented in a gradual way and, most of all, if political elites commit themselves to the preservation of democracy above and beyond the achievement of any other goal.

NOTES

Chapter 1

1. For details on Goulart's program of "basic reforms" see Thomas E. Skidmore, *Politics in Brazil, 1930–1964: An Experiment in Democracy* (New York: Oxford University Press, 1967); Peter Flynn, *Brazil: A Political Analysis* (Boulder: Westview Press, 1983); Carlos Castelo Branco, *Introdução à Revolução de 1964* (Rio de Janeiro: Artenova, 1975); Afonso Arinos de Melo Franco, *Evolução da Crise Brasileira* (São Paulo: Editora Nacional, 1965); Abelardo Jurema, *Sexta-Feira 13: Os Ultimos Dias do Governo João Goulart* (Rio de Janeiro: Ed. O Cruzeiro, 1964); Cibilis da Rocha Viana, *Reformas de Base e a Política Nacionalista de Desenvolvimento—De Getúlio a Jango* (Rio de Janeiro: Civilização Brasileira, 1980); Moniz Bandeira, *O Governo João Goulart* (Rio de Janeiro: Civilização Brasileira, 1978). Discussions of Allende's program of reforms can be found in Paul E. Sigmund, *The Overthrow of Allende and the Politics of Chile, 1964–1976* (Pittsburgh: University of Pittsburgh Press, 1977); Arturo Valenzuela, *The Breakdown of Democratic Regimes: Chile* (Baltimore: Johns Hopkins University Press, 1978); Arturo Valenzuela and J. Samuel Valenzuela, eds., *Chile: Politics and Society* (New Brunswick: Transaction, 1976); Ann Zammit, ed., *The Chilean Way to Socialism* (Austin: University of Texas Press, 1973); Stefan de Vylder, *Allende's Chile: The Political Economy of the Rise and Fall of the Unidad Popular* (Cambridge: Cambridge University Press, 1976); Philip O'Brien, ed., *Allende's Chile* (New York: Praeger, 1976).

2. For the events leading to the fall of Goulart, see Alfred Stepan, *The Military in Politics: Changing Patterns in Brazil* (Princeton: Princeton University Press, 1971); Alfred Stepan, "Political Leadership and Regime Breakdown: Brazil," in Juan J. Linz and Alfred Stepan, eds., *The Breakdown of Democratic Regimes* (Baltimore: Johns Hopkins University Press, 1978), pp. 110–37; Skidmore, *Politics in Brazil;* Peter Flynn, *Brazil: A Political Analysis.*

3. On the fall of Allende's government, see Sigmund, *The Overthrow of Allende and Chile's Politics;* Valenzuela, *The Breakdown of Democratic Regimes: Chile;* De Vylder, *Allende's Chile.*

4. The controversy is centered around the adequacy of structural-economic explanations and the relative explanatory weights of economic and political structures. To my knowledge, the only study that

explicitly criticizes structural explanations for disregarding intentional phenomena is Argelina M. C. Figueiredo, "Political Coalitions in Brazil, 1961–1964: Alternatives to Political Crisis," Ph.D. diss. (University of Chicago, 1987). For extensive discussions of the controversy, see the several papers in David Collier, ed., *The New Authoritarianism in Latin America* (Princeton: Princeton University Press, 1979); Youssef Cohen, "Democracy from Above: The Political Origins of Military Dictatorship in Brazil," *World Politics* 40 (1987): 30–50; Figueiredo, "Political Coalitions in Brazil," chap. 1.

5. Structural explanations of this kind were first based on Marxist-oriented theories of imperialism. Recent variations have relied on dependency theory. According to these explanations, at an advanced stage of capitalist development, dependent countries are prone to suffer from structural crises which threaten capitalist accumulation. To maintain the capitalist system a shift to more authoritarian forms of the state is required. For some of the most prominent explanations of this sort, see Celso Furtado, *Análise do Modêlo Brasileiro* (Rio: Civilização Brasileira, 1972); Rui M. Marini, *Subdesarollo y Revolución* (Mexico City: Siglo Vientiuno); Rui M. Marini, *Dialética de la Dependencia* (Mexico City: Nueva Era, 1973); Guillermo A. O'Donnell, *Modernization and Bureaucratic-Authoritarianism* (Berkeley: Institute of International Studies, University of California, 1973); O'Donnell, "Corporatism and the Question of the State," in James M. Malloy, ed., *Authoritarianism and Corporatism in Latin America* (Pittsburgh: University of Pittsburgh Press, 1977), pp. 47–87; O'Donnell, "Reflections on the Patterns of Change in the Bureaucratic-Authoritarian State," *Latin American Research Review* 13 (1978): 3–38; O'Donnell, "Tensions in the Bureaucratic-Authoritarian State and the Question of Democracy," in David Collier, *The New Authoritarianism in Latin America.*

6. There are three basic versions of the economic explanation. Each emphasizes a different feature of dependent capitalist, or import-substituting, industrialization. One of them argues that ultimately authoritarian regimes are the result of the limits imposed by a high concentration of income on the size of the market for luxury goods. A second sees authoritarian regimes as the result of a need to "deepen" developing economies. Finally, the third version sees those regimes as the result of a need to effect a transition to more orthodox, market-oriented, policies. For the first version, see, for instance, Kenneth P. Erickson and Patrick V. Peppe, "Dependent Capitalist Development, U.S. Foreign Policy, and Repression of the Working Class in Chile and Brazil," *Latin American Perspectives* 3 (1976): 19–44; Furtado, *Análise do Modêlo Brasileiro.* For the second, see O'Donnell, *Modernization and Bureaucratic-Authoritarianism.* For the third version, see A. O. Hirschman, "The Turn to Authoritarianism in Latin America and the Search for Its Eco-

nomic Determinants," in David Collier, ed., *The New Authoritarianism in Latin America;* Thomas E. Skidmore, "Politics and Economic Policy Making in Authoritarian Brazil, 1937–1971," in Alfred Stepan, ed., *Authoritarian Brazil* (New Haven: Yale University Press, 1973), pp. 3–46; Skidmore, "The Politics of Economic Stabilization in Postwar Latin America," in James M. Malloy, *Authoritarianism and Corporatism in Latin America,* pp. 149–90. I shall deal with these and other economic explanations in great detail in chapter 3 of this book.

7. For an exhaustive discussion of the potential relationship between strictly political variables and the collapse of democratic institutions, see Juan J. Linz, *The Breakdown of Democratic Regimes: Crisis, Breakdown, and Reequilibration* (Baltimore: Johns Hopkins University Press, 1979), pp. 14–74. Studies stressing political factors have relied on Sartori's model of "polarized pluralism." See Giovanni Sartori, "European Political Parties: The Case of Polarized Pluralism," in Joseph LaPalombara, ed., *Political Parties and Political Development* (Princeton: Princeton University Press, 1966). The most systematic empirical study showing that the polarization of a multiparty system can lead to the breakdown of democracy can be found in Wanderley G. dos Santos, "The Calculus of Conflict: Impasse in Brazilian Politics and the Crisis of 1964," Ph.D. diss. (Stanford University, 1979). For an account of the Chilean breakdown that relies on Sartori's model, see Valenzuela, *The Breakdown of Democratic Regimes: Chile.* For a study of the Chilean collapse that focuses on political factors, see Paul E. Sigmund, *The Overthrow of Allende and the Politics of Chile.*

8. These are by and large empirical critiques, that is, critiques concerned with how well the explanation fits all of the relevant facts. With one exception, these critiques hardly deal with the theoretical and logical problems of structural explanations of democratic collapse. As I will show in chapter 3, this neglect of theoretical and logical issues has generated a great deal of confusion. For some excellent empirical critiques, see A. O. Hirschman, "The Turn to Authoritarianism in Latin America and the Search for Its Economic Determinants"; José Serra, "Three Mistaken Theses Regarding the Connection between Industrialization and Authoritarian Regimes," in David Collier, ed., *The New Authoritarianism in Latin America,* pp. 99–163; Robert Kaufman, "Industrial Change and Authoritarian Rule in Latin America: A Concrete Review of the Bureaucratic-Authoritarian Model," in Collier, ed., pp. 165–254.

9. To my knowledge, the only scholar who has explicitly recognized some of the logical and theoretical problems of structural explanations of the breakdown of authoritarian regimes is Argelina Figueiredo. In her study of the Brazilian breakdown she criticizes structural explanations of the Brazilian case for neglecting the intentions of the major actors involved in the events leading to the coup of 1964, and for implying

that those events and the coup were inevitable. See Figueiredo, "Political Coalitions in Brazil, 1961–1964."

10. Structural explanations predominate not only in the explanation of the collapse of democracy but also in the explanation of a variety of other large-scale political transformations. Since the early seventies, structural explanations of political change have become increasingly dominant in the United States. Previously, structural explanations had fallen into disuse because of their reductionism, that is, because they tended to give excessive explanatory weight to socioeconomic factors at the expense of political structures. The new brand of structural explanation has incorporated political structures successfully in the explanation of a wide variety of political phenomena. For a defense of this new structuralism, as well as for a long list of studies based on this framework, see Theda Skocpol, "Bringing the State Back In: Strategies of Analysis in Current Research," in Peter B. Evans, D. Rueschemeyer, and Theda Skocpol, eds., *Bringing the State Back In* (Cambridge: Cambridge University Press, 1985).

11. Structural explanations have been criticized for failing to specify the causal mechanisms linking structures to the outcomes they are supposed to explain, and for relying on faulty forms of functional explanation. This does not mean, of course, that it is impossible to specify such mechanisms. Although structural explanations usually do not specify them, a few rational-choice theorists have shown that, under certain limited conditions, it is possible to define the causal mechanism linking structural conditions to the outcome being explained. However, as I will argue in the next chapter, in a great number of cases, structural explanations are unlikely to succeed. In any event, to be successful, structural explanations must show, rather than assume, that structures do in fact cause the action and interaction that leads to the outcome being explained. Before disposing of intentional phenomena, proponents of structural explanations must demonstrate that there is no need to incorporate such phenomena in their explanations. On this issue, see Michael Taylor, "Rationality and Revolutionary Collective Action," in Taylor, ed., *Rationality and Revolution* (Cambridge: Cambridge University Press, 1988), pp. 63–97, and Jon Elster, *Ulysses and the Sirens* (Cambridge: Cambridge University Press, 1979).

12. For lack of a better term, I borrow the label "intentional" from Jon Elster to denote explanations that rely on intentions as the causes of action. This label is a bit confusing because it suggests that all outcomes being explained must have been intended, which would rule out unintended outcomes—a large part of social life. But the label "intentional explanation" need not be understood in this way. It is meant to refer to individual intentions as the *ultimate* causes of social outcomes. A complete intentional explanation, however, must incorporate not only

individual action but also the strategic interaction that mediates between intentional action and the final outcome being explained. Intentional explanation will be examined in greater detail in chapters 4 and 5 of this book. For the distinction between causal, functional, and intentional explanation, see Jon Elster, *Explaining Technical Change* (Cambridge: Cambridge University Press, 1982), pp. 1–100.

13. In defense of structural explanation, it has been argued that intentions and strategic action are irrelevant in the explanation of large-scale transformations because these are largely unintended. Theda Skocpol, for instance, has argued that only structural explanations can account for social revolutions, since these are not the result of purposive action; revolutionary outcomes are not intended or foreseen by anyone. But this is no reason to reject intentional explanations of revolutions. On the contrary, a type of intentional explanation—rational-choice explanation—is especially well suited to the study of revolutions. One of the major successes of rational-choice theory is its solution of the problems posed by the unintended consequences of action. For Skocpol's argument see her *States and Social Revolutions: A Comparative Analysis of France, Russia, and China* (Cambridge: Cambridge University Press, 1979), pp. 14–18. For a demonstration of the applicability of rational-choice theory to the study of revolutions, see Michael Taylor, "Rationality and Revolutionary Collective Action." For interesting discussions of the problem of unintended consequences, see Jon Elster, *Nuts and Bolts for the Social Sciences* (Cambridge: Cambridge University Press, 1989), pp. 91–100, and Raymond Boudon, *The Unintended Consequences of Social Action* (New York: St. Martin's Press, 1981).

14. Intentional explanations need not rely on rational choice. Nonrational action may be the basis of an intentional explanation. This is the case, for instance, when individuals deliberately choose to act according to norms without calculating the advantages or disadvantages that may result from acting in this as opposed to other ways. For the several types of intentional explanation, see Jon Elster, *Explaining Technical Change,* pp. 62–90. For irrational and nonrational action, see Elster, *Ulysses and the Sirens;* Elster, *Sour Grapes* (Cambridge: Cambridge University Press, 1985); Elster, *The Cement of Society* (Cambridge: Cambridge University Press, 1989).

15. For a survey of the literature on rational-choice explanation, see Jon Elster, "Introduction," in Elster, ed., *Rational Choice* (New York: New York University Press, 1986).

16. This does not mean that the role of rational-choice theory is merely to provide the link between structural conditions and historical outcome, that is, to flesh out structural explanations. This is clearly not the case because, as I pointed out, although structures influence preferences and beliefs, they do not necessarily determine them. Pure individu-

alists argue that the causes of beliefs and preferences are themselves nothing but properties of individuals, and that structures are *nothing but* stable individual interactions. As I shall argue in the next chapter, however, intentional explanation need not require a commitment to the extreme individualist position usually referred to as *methodological individualism.* My position is close to that of Michael Taylor, who has recently argued for a methodological perspective which is both *individualist and structuralist.* See Michael Taylor, "Rationality and Revolutionary Collective Action," esp. pp. 93–97.

17. As Ordeshook has put it, "Game theory is about how people condition their decisions on the decisions of others when they believe that others are doing the same." Peter C. Ordeshook, *Game Theory and Political Theory* (Cambridge: Cambridge University Press, 1986), p. 97.

18. For some of this evidence, see Figueiredo, "Political Coalitions in Brazil, 1961–1964," chap. 4; Valenzuela, *The Breakdown of Democratic Regimes: Chile,* chaps. 2, 3. For a more detailed discussion, see chapters 6 and 7 of this book.

19. The literature on the prisoner's dilemma is very large. For some recent works relevant to political scientists, see Michael Taylor, *Anarchy and Cooperation* (London: Wiley, 1976); Taylor, *The Possibility of Cooperation* (Cambridge: Cambridge University Press, 1987); Robert Axelrod, *The Evolution of Cooperation* (New York: Basic Books, 1984).

Chapter 2

1. For the most extreme form of methodological individualism see F. A. Hayek, *The Counter-Revolution of Science: Studies on the Abuse of Reason* (Glencoe: Free Press, 1952), chaps. 4, 6, and 8; K. R. Popper, *The Open Society and Its Enemies* (London: Routledge and Kegan Paul, 1945), chap. 14; K. R. Popper, *The Poverty of Historicism* (London: Routledge and Kegan Paul, 1957), chaps. 7, 23, 24, and 31. For an excellent discussion and critique of methodological individualism, see Steven Lukes, "Methodological Individualism Reconsidered," in Dorothy Emmet and Alasdair MacIntyre, eds., *Sociological Theory and Philosophical Analysis* (New York: Macmillan, 1970), pp. 76–88. Michael Taylor has recently criticized extreme forms of methodological individualism, arguing that, although structures emerge as the result of the actions of individuals (structures are "precipitates" of past intentional actions), structures are not the same thing as these actions. Individuals and structures should therefore be accorded the same explanatory status. See Michael Taylor, "Rationality and Revolutionary Collective Action," in M. Taylor, ed., *Rationality and Revolution* (Cambridge: Cambridge University Press, 1988), pp. 93–97. For other political scientists who advocate a rational-choice approach that is both individualist and struc-

turalist, see Robert H. Bates, *Essays on the Political Economy of Rural Africa* (Berkeley: University of California Press, 1987); Margaret Levi, *Of Rule and Revenue* (Berkeley: University of California Press, 1988); Adam Przeworski, "Marxism and Rational Choice," *Politics and Society* 14 (1985): 379–409.

2. Jon Elster, *Ulysses and the Sirens: Studies in Rationality and Irrationality* (Cambridge: Cambridge University Press, 1979), p. 113. For interesting discussions of the logic of structural explanation and of explanation in the social sciences see also Elster, *Ulysses and the Sirens,* pp. 112–17; Elster, *Explaining Technical Change* (Cambridge: Cambridge University Press, 1983).

3. Under some circumstances, it may in fact be the case that actors have practically no choice but to act in ways dictated by the structural situation. But this does not mean that actors never have any choice. To prove that this is generally true, as structuralists seem to assume, structuralists would have to specify a general causal mechanism showing how structures determine action. To date, no one has come up with this general mechanism. Alternatively, some structuralists have argued that since human preferences are roughly always similar, it is always possible to predict choice and action on the basis of structure. Again, under some circumstances, it is possible to presume that preferences will be the same. But I am sure no one would want to presume that, given a set of circumstances, human beings will always prefer to do the same thing. For a discussion of the conditions under which one could assume uniformity of preferences, see Michael Taylor, "Rationality and Revolutionary Collective Action," pp. 90–93. For a general discussion on structuralist strategies of explanation, see Elster, *Ulysses and the Sirens,* chap. 3.

4. Skocpol's methodological position is avowedly structural. She chastises other influential approaches, such as Tilly's, which incorporate political goals and strategies, for being excessively "voluntaristic." According to her, the intentions of revolutionaries and of other actors are irrelevant to the explanation of social revolutions because no one *makes* revolutions; no matter what the actors wanted, revolutions could only occur under certain special structural conditions. Even if this were true, however, it does not follow (as I show later in this chapter) that an explanation of revolution can avoid referring to the preferences, intentions, and choices of the actors involved. For Skocpol's methodological position, see Theda Skocpol, *States and Social Revolutions: A Comparative Analysis of France, Russia, and China* (Cambridge: Cambridge University Press, 1979), pp. 14–18; Skocpol, *Vision and Method in Historical Sociology* (Cambridge: Cambridge University Press, 1984). For Tilly's alternative view, see Charles Tilly, "Revolutions and Collective Violence," in F. I. Greenstein and N. W. Polsby, eds., *Handbook of Political Science* (Reading: Addison-Wesley, 1975), pp. 483–556. Another well-

known structuralist explanation of revolutions is Jeffery M. Paige, *Agrarian Revolution: Social Movements and Export Agriculture in the Underdeveloped World* (New York: Free Press, 1975). For an interesting comment on structural explanations of political change, see A. O. Hirschman, *Rival Views of Market Society* (New York: Viking, 1986), pp. 171–82.

5. Skocpol does not analyze the choices available to those actors in order to demonstrate that they chose according to their interests. She seems to assume implicitly that interests are transparent and that, given these fairly obvious interests, structural conditions unambiguously and uniquely determine the choices people actually make. People mechanically act according to their interests. Hence the explanatory irrelevance of beliefs and preferences. This is a common strategy among structuralists, but it is not the only one. Other structuralists assume that people act according to their values rather than their interests. In this case the structural situation compels them to act according to the ways in which they were socialized. Structure determines both people's values and the particular ways in which they act. See note 29.

6. The recent literature on the French Revolution, for instance, puts into question many structuralist arguments concerning social revolutions. Inspired by Alfred Cobban's work, the new revisionist literature has challenged not only the Marxist interpretation of the French Revolution but also most of the structural and functional arguments on the subject. It questions the conjecture that the revolution was a bourgeois revolution. According to the revisionists, the revolution was neither brought about nor led by the bourgeoisie, nor was it necessary to unfetter a nascent capitalism from its feudal shackles. Some go so far as to argue that the effect of the revolution, if any, was to *slow down* the development of industrial capitalism. There is also a great deal of evidence suggesting that the revolution was far from inevitable; that the monarchy and its ministers had the power to avoid the revolution. See Alfred A. Cobban, *The Social Interpretation of the French Revolution* (Cambridge: Cambridge University Press, 1964); G. V. Taylor, "Noncapitalist Wealth and the Origins of the French Revolution," *American Historical Review* 79 (1967): 469–96; François Furet, *Interpreting the French Revolution* (Cambridge: Cambridge University Press, 1981); William Doyle, *Origins of the French Revolution* (Oxford: Oxford University Press, 1980); Doyle, *The Oxford History of the French Revolution* (Oxford: Oxford University Press, 1990); T. C. W. Blanning, *The French Revolution: Aristocrats versus Bourgeois?* (London, 1988); G. Comminel, *Rethinking the French Revolution: Marxism and the Revisionist Challenge* (London, 1987); Lynn Hunt, *Politics, Culture, and Class in the French Revolution* (Berkeley: University of California Press, 1984); Simon Schama, *Citizens: A Chronicle of the French Revolution*

(New York: Knopf, 1989); E. J. Hobsbawm, *Echoes of the Marseillaise: Two Centuries Look Back on the French Revolution* (New Brunswick: Rutgers University Press, 1990).

7. Michael Taylor, for instance, has shown how revolutionary collective action is the product of rational action. He explains revolutionary action by drawing on the theory of collective action developed by Olson and Hardin, and on the theory of conditional cooperation developed by himself and other game theorists. See Mancur Olson, *The Logic of Collective Action* (Cambridge: Harvard University Press, 1965); Russell Hardin, *Collective Action* (Baltimore: Johns Hopkins University Press, 1982); Michael Taylor, *Community, Anarchy, and Liberty* (Cambridge: Cambridge University Press, 1982); Taylor, *The Possibility of Cooperation* (Cambridge: Cambridge University Press, 1987); Taylor, "Rationality and Revolutionary Collective Action."

8. Two mistakes are involved in this inference. First, causality is illegitimately inferred from correlation. And second, an effect is confused with a cause. This does not mean that effects cannot be causes. As we shall see, consequences can be the causes of social phenomena. But a causal feedback loop connecting the consequence of a phenomenon back to it in a reinforcing manner must be specified before the consequence may be legitimately thought of as a cause of that phenomenon.

9. According to Elster, the deep-seated belief that our social world must make sense has its roots in two traditions in the history of ideas. The first is the theological tradition that culminated with the idea that "all the apparent evils in the world have beneficial consequences for the larger patterns that justify and explain them," and the "strong presumption that private vices will turn out to be public benefits" (Elster, *Explaining Technical Change*, p. 56). The second root of the belief that social phenomena must make sense is modern biology. Darwinian biology gave biological adaptation a firm scientific basis; it showed that one did not have to rely on a divine creator to find meaning in biological phenomena. As such, it inspired those who sought to impart scientific meaning to the workings of human society. As Elster notes, however, the presumption that the adaptation and stability of the animal world carries over to society does not seem to be justified. See Elster, *Explaining Technical Change*, chap. 2.

10. The more extreme version can be traced back to Mandeville. It was rejected by Merton, who argued for the more moderate version of the functionalist paradigm. See Robert K. Merton, "Manifest and Latent Functions," in R. K. Merton, *On Theoretical Sociology* (New York: Free Press, 1967), pp. 73–138. For a discussion of the fallacy in Merton's version, see Elster, *Ulysses and the Sirens*, pp. 28–35; Elster, *Explaining Technical Change*, 57–68; Elster, "Marxism, Functionalism, and Game Theory," *Theory and Society* 11 (1982): 453–82.

11. In Darwinian biology natural selection is the impersonal causal mechanism that gives meaning and purpose to organic phenomena. This general mechanism therefore imparts validity to functionalist explanations in biology. But there is no equivalent general mechanism in the social sciences. Therefore, the presumption that social processes are guided by a purpose but not by purposive actors is of doubtful validity.

12. The actors who unintentionally bring about the beneficial consequences are not necessarily the same as those who benefit from them. For example, one could argue that the military in Latin American countries have established military regimes that have had beneficial consequences for capitalists. In this case, the military bring about the consequences which also benefit the capitalist class. In addition to requiring that those who benefit from some social structure do not recognize its beneficial effects, this more complex form of functional explanation requires that the actors who bring that structure about do so unintentionally. In our example, the military would establish an authoritarian regime for reasons other than the protection of capitalism, and the capitalists would not recognize the beneficial effect of the military regime on the capitalist economy (they might even sincerely oppose authoritarianism). For this complex form of functionalism, see Elster, *Explaining Technical Change,* p. 57.

13. The example is taken from Bronislaw Malinowski, *Magic, Science, and Religion* (Boston: Beacon Press). See Arthur L. Stinchcombe, *Constructing Social Theories* (New York: Harcourt, Brace, and World, 1968), p. 83. Elster criticizes Stinchcombe's account of functional explanation. The disagreement revolves around types of social selection processes and the possibility of a general causal mechanism that can justify in principle functionalist thought in the social sciences. For Stinchcombe's position, see Stinchcombe, *Constructing Social Theories,* pp. 80–101; Stinchcombe, "Merton's Theory of Social Structure," in L. Coser, ed., *The Idea of a Social Structure: Papers in Honor of Robert Merton* (Harcourt Brace Jovanovich, 1974); Stinchcombe, "Is the Prisoner's Dilemma All of Sociology?" *Inquiry* 23 (1980): 187–92. For Elster's critique, see Elster, *Ulysses and the Sirens,* pp. 32–33; Elster, *Explaining Technical Change,* pp. 61–64.

14. I am here borrowing from Flaubert, who, commenting on human conceit, said, "People believe a little too easily that the function of the sun is to help the cabbages along." Quoted in Julian Barnes, *Flaubert's Parrot* (London: Picador, 1985), p. 162.

15. Lewis Coser, "Social Conflict and the Theory of Social Change," in C. G. Smith, ed., *Conflict Resolution: Contributions of the Behavioral Sciences* (Notre Dame: University of Notre Dame Press, 1971), p. 60. Quoted in Elster, *Explaining Technical Change,* p. 59.

16. Or, alternatively, should those who bring about conflict be dif-

ferent from those who benefit from its consequences, Coser would have to show how the first bring conflict about without intending to do so, and he would have to demonstrate that the beneficiaries of the conflict do not recognize its beneficial consequences. See discussion in note 12.

17. I here follow Elster's distinctions among objective teleology, subjective teleology, and teleonomy. The first is a process guided by a purpose without an intentional subject, the second designates intentional acts with an intentional subject, and the third refers to adaptive behavior brought about by natural selection. While both objective teleology and teleonomy refer to processes with a purpose but without an intentional subject, objective teleology is not a valid way of thinking about human societies because there is no general mechanism equivalent to natural selection allowing the presumption that social phenomena can be explained by their consequences. See notes 9, 10, and 11, and Elster, "Marxism, Functionalism, and Game Theory," p. 455.

18. Marx's ideas on Bonapartism are mainly in Karl Marx, *The Eighteenth Brumaire of Louis Bonaparte* (New York: International Publishers, 1963). His ideas on Bonapartism and the capitalist state were fully developed into a structural theory of the state by Poulantzas, who offered a functionalist structural explanation of the relative autonomy of the state in capitalist society. Poulantzas explicitly criticized Marxists who saw the capitalist state merely as the instrument of the capitalist class (the so-called instrumental theory of the state). For the instrumental theories see Ralph Miliband, *The State in Capitalist Society* (New York: Basic Books, 1969). For the functional theory of the state, see Nicos Poulantzas, "The Problem of the Capitalist State," *New Left Review* 58 (1969): 67–78; Poulantzas, *Political Power and Social Classes* (London: New Left Books, 1974); Poulantzas, *Classes in Contemporary Capitalism* (London: New Left Books, 1975); Poulantzas, *Fascism and Dictatorship* (London: New Left Books, 1974). Also see Miliband's reply to Poulantzas in Miliband, "The Capitalist State: Reply to Nicos Poulantzas," *New Left Review* 59 (1970), and Miliband, "Poulantzas and the Capitalist State," *New Left Review* 92 (1973): 83–92. For exhaustive reviews of the literature on the theory of the capitalist state, see Bob Jessop, *Theories of the State* (New York: New York University Press, 1983), and Martin Carnoy, *The State and Political Theory* (Princeton: Princeton University Press, 1984).

19. For an interesting discussion of the several possible interpretations of Marx's explanation of Bonapartism, see Jon Elster, *Making Sense of Marx* (Cambridge: Cambridge University Press, 1985), pp. 411–28, and Elster, "Marxism, Functionalism, and Game Theory," pp. 458–59.

20. Or, alternatively, Marx should have shown how some other group unintentionally brings about noncapitalist governments that ben-

efit the capitalists. In this case, he would also have had to show that the capitalists do not recognize the beneficial consequences of these forms of government (or, at least, that they do not recognize the causal relation between those governments and their beneficial consequences). See notes 12 and 16.

21. Because of some ambiguities in Marx's writings, it would seem to be possible to interpret his explanation as an intentional one. Such an interpretation, however, is incompatible with the structural and functional thrust of Marx's argument. One cannot say that Bonapartism is the result of the strategic action of capitalists and at the same time suggest that Bonapartism is explained by its functions for capitalism. The first argument implies that capitalists intentionally established a noncapitalist government, while the second implies that Bonapartism was an unintended consequence of the actions of those who brought it about. See Elster, "Marxism, Functionalism, and Game Theory," p. 458.

22. The indirect strategy here consists in forgoing power in the present to gain greater power in the future: one step backward to make two steps forward. A functional explanation can never invoke such strategic behavior, because future benefits can never prevail over present ones in the absence of an intentional actor. To the extent that Marx alluded to a trade-off between present and future, even though his explanation is essentially a functionalist structural one, his explanation of Bonapartism is clearly inconsistent. For the inconsistencies of "long-term functionalism," see Elster, "Marxism, Functionalism, and Game Theory," pp. 458–59.

23. Recently, however, theorists with a Marxist orientation have begun to recognize the limitations of functional theories of the state. As a consequence, there have been some attempts to develop more adequate functional theories, and some attempts to elaborate nonfunctional theories of the state. With very few exceptions, these theorists do not include beliefs, preferences, or intentions in their explanations. The small minority that has tried to cast Marxism in an intentional framework, in order to establish its microfoundations, has so changed Marxist theory as to make it almost unrecognizable. For some of the recent work on the theory of the state, see Claus Offe, "The Capitalist State and the Problem of Policy Formation," in L. N. Lindberg, R. Alford, C. Crouch, and C. Offe, eds., *Stress and Contradiction in Modern Capitalism* (Lexington: D. C. Heath, 1973); Offe, "Structural Problems of the Capitalist State: Class Rule and the Political System. On the Selectiveness of Political Institutions," in Klaus Von Bayme, ed., *German Political Studies* (Beverly Hills: Sage, 1974); Offe, "Theses on the Theory of the State," *New German Critique* 6 (1975): 137–47; Fred Block, *Revising State Theory: Essays in Politics and Postindustrialism* (Philadelphia: Temple University Press, 1987); Goran Therborn, *What Does the Ruling Class*

Do When It Rules? (London: New Left Books, 1978); D. Gold, C. Lo, and E. O. Wright, "Recent Developments in Marxist Theories of the State," *Monthly Review* 27 (1975): 29–43, 36–51; Martin Carnoy, *The State and Political Theory.*

24. See John Foster, *Class Struggle and the Industrial Revolution* (London: Methuen, 1974); E. P. Thompson, "The Moral Economy of the English Crowd in the Eighteenth Century," *Past and Present* 50 (1971); James O'Connor, *The Fiscal Crisis of the State* (New York: St. Martin's, 1973); S. Bowles and Herbert Gintis, *Schooling in Capitalist America* (London: Routledge and Kegan Paul, 1976). For Elster's critique, see "Marxism, Functionalism, and Game Theory," pp. 454–63.

25. For Malinowski, Merton, and Coser, see notes 10, 13, and 17. For a discussion of functionalism in the thought of Foucault and Bourdieu, see Elster, "Marxism, Functionalism, and Game Theory," pp. 460–61.

26. Elster, *Explaining Technical Change*, chap. 2.

27. There are good reasons to believe that, although most functional explanations have been flawed, there is far more room for functional explanation than Elster is willing to concede. For this argument, see Russell Hardin, "Rationality, Irrationality, and Functional Explanation," *Social Science Information* 19 (1980): 775–82.

28. G. A. Cohen has argued that, although Marxists have so far been unable to specify causal mechanisms for their functional explanations, their explanations are still valid. He argues that, as long as these explanations satisfy the requirements of consequence laws, they do not have to provide a causal mechanism to have validity. But Elster has convincingly shown that Cohen's argument is flawed. See G. A. Cohen, "Functional Explanation, Consequence Explanation, and Marxism," *Inquiry* 25 (1982): 27–56; Elster, *Explaining Technical Change,* pp. 64–68.

29. Structural explanations following what Brian Barry calls the "sociological" tradition assume that people internalize the values inherent in social structures and mechanically act according to those values. Those following what Barry calls the "economic" school, including Marxists, impute objective interests to actors according to their structural position. For the problems of both of these approaches, see Brian Barry, *Sociologists, Economists, and Democracy* (Chicago: University of Chicago Press, 1978); Dennis Wrong, "The Oversocialized Conception of Man in Modern Sociology," *American Sociological Review* 26 (1961): 183–93; Christopher Lloyd, *Explanation in Social History* (New York: Basil Blackwell, 1986).

30. This is the problem with nonfunctionalist structural explanation. The problem is not so much that these explanations implicitly impute values and interests. To some extent, all explanations do so. Structuralists, however, do not examine their imputations.

31. This problem came to the attention of sociologists and political scientists through Olson's work on the logic of collective action. See Mancur Olson, Jr., *The Logic of Collective Action* (Cambridge: Harvard University Press, 1961). See also Russell Hardin, *Collective Action* (Baltimore: Johns Hopkins University Press, 1982).

32. Skocpol, *States and Social Revolutions,* chap. 3. Skocpol is not alone in stressing the importance of community for peasant rebellions. A great number of historians have done so. For some examples, see Taylor, "Rationality and Revolutionary Collective Action."

33. Taylor shows that Skocpol's explanation is perfectly compatible with a rational-choice explanation. His explanation goes far beyond Skocpol's, for it explains precisely how community favors rebellion. It is important to note that though in this case structural and intentional explanation are compatible, in other cases a close examination of intentional phenomena may refute the structural explanation as implausible. Examples of the latter are given in the next chapter of this book. See Taylor, "Rationality and Revolutionary Collective Action."

34. Ibid., p. 76.

35. To be more precise, Taylor argues that it was "thin-rational" for peasants to rebel. The thin theory of rationality, which provides the foundation for conventional microeconomic theory, has as its basic features the assumptions that rationality is relative to given beliefs, that the agent is egoistic, and that the range of incentives to affect the agent is limited. See ibid.

36. Ibid., p. 67.

37. Ibid., pp. 95–97.

38. Also worth noting is the fact that the initial structural conditions themselves ultimately have to be explained, and that they cannot be explained without reference to actors and their beliefs, preferences, and intentions. This does not mean, however, that structures can be reduced to interactions among individuals. I agree with Taylor, who argues that, although structures emerge as the result of the actions of individuals, they are not the same thing as these actions, and that structures are best conceptualized as "*precipitates* of past intentional actions." Ibid., p. 97.

Chapter 3

1. An alternative, equivalent, way of saying this is that, with the "exhaustion," or crisis, of the easy phase of import-substituting industrialization, the populist class coalition could no longer survive. The populist class compromise was possible because of the exuberant growth of the easy phase; with the decline in growth, the lower classes had to be excluded both politically and economically. This is how Furtado, Cardoso, O'Donnell, and Erickson see it. See Celso Furtado, "Political Obstacles to the Economic Development of Brazil," in Claudio Veliz, ed., *Obsta-*

cles to Change in Latin America (London: Oxford University Press, 1965); Fernando H. Cardoso, "Associated Dependent Development: Theoretical and Practical Implications," in A. Stepan, ed., *Authoritarian Brazil* (New Haven: Yale University Press, 1973); Guillermo A. O'Donnell, *Modernization and Bureaucratic-Authoritarianism* (Berkeley: Institute of International Studies, University of California, 1973), pp. 55–69; Kenneth P. Erickson, *The Brazilian Corporative State and Working-Class Politics* (Berkeley: University of California Press, 1977), p. 10. Still another way of expressing this thesis is Stepan's; he maintains that the crisis leading to the Brazilian coup was due to rising demands from the masses when the rate of growth was declining; or, as he puts it, to an increase in the loads of the "distributive capability" of the Brazilian system when its "extractive capability" was decreasing. See Alfred Stepan, *The Military in Politics* (Princeton: Princeton University Press, 1971), pp. 134–40; Alfred Stepan, *The State and Society: Peru in Comparative Perspective* (Princeton: Princeton University Press, 1978), pp. 79–80. Thus, this thesis is shared even by explanations like Stepan's, which give almost equal weight to economic and political factors. The problem with Stepan's otherwise excellent books is that they still give too much weight to economic factors and never really deal with the causal connections between the economic and the political. For a critique, see Youssef Cohen, "Democracy from Above: The Political Origins of Military Dictatorship in Brazil," *World Politics* 40 (1987): 30–54. For other similar structural accounts of the links between capitalist development and democracy, see Peter Evans, *Dependent Development* (Princeton: Princeton University Press, 1979); J. Stephens, E. H. Stephens, and Dietrich Reuschemeyer, *Capitalist Development and Democracy* (Chicago: University of Chicago Press, 1992).

2. Fernando Henrique Cardoso, "Associated-Dependent Development"; Celso Furtado, *Análise do Modêlo Brasileiro* (Rio: Civilização Brasileira, 1972); Rui Mauro Marini, *Subdesarollo y Revolución* (Mexico City: Siglo Vientiuno, 1969); *Dialéctica de la Dependencia* (Mexico City: Nueva Era, 1973); Kenneth P. Erickson and Patrick V. Peppe, "Dependent Capitalist Development, U.S. Foreign Policy, and Repression of the Working Class in Chile and Brazil," *Latin American Perspectives* 3 (1976): 19–44.

3. Guillermo A. O'Donnell, *Modernization and Bureaucratic-Authoritarianism;* O'Donnell, "Corporatism and the Question of the State," in James M. Malloy, ed., *Authoritarianism and Corporatism in Latin America* (Pittsburgh: University of Pittsburgh Press, 1977), pp. 47–87; O'Donnell, "Reflections on the Patterns of Change in the Bureaucratic-Authoritarian State," *Latin American Research Review* 13 (1978): 3–38; O'Donnell, "Tensions in the Bureaucratic-Authoritarian State and the Question of Democracy," in David Collier, ed., *The New*

Authoritarianism in Latin America (Princeton: Princeton University Press, 1979), pp. 285–318.

4. For different (though related) variations of this argument, see A. O. Hirschman, "The Turn to Authoritarianism in Latin America and the Search for Its Economic Determinants," in David Collier, ed., *The New Authoritarianism in Latin America,* pp. 72–79; Thomas E. Skidmore, "Politics and Economic Policy Making in Authoritarian Brazil, 1937–71," in A. Stepan, ed., *Authoritarian Brazil,* pp. 3–46; Skidmore, "The Politics of Economic Stabilization in Postwar Latin America," in James M. Malloy, ed., *Authoritarianism and Corporatism in Latin America,* pp. 149–90; Michael Wallerstein, "The Collapse of Democracy in Brazil," *Latin American Research Review* 15 (1980): 3–40; John Sheehan, "Market-Oriented Economic Policies and Political Repression in Latin America," *Economic Development and Cultural Change* 28 (1980): 264–89. See also David Pion-Berlin, "Political Repression and Economic Doctrines," *Comparative Political Studies* 16 (1983): 37–66; Youssef Cohen, "The Impact of Bureaucratic-Authoritarian Rule on Economic Growth," *Comparative Political Studies* 18 (1985): 123–36.

5. For greater detail on the functioning of this mechanism, see Albert O. Hirschman, "The Political Economy of Import-Substituting Industrialization in Latin America," in Hirschman, *A Bias for Hope* (New Haven: Yale University Press, 1971), pp. 85–123, esp. p. 117.

6. See A. O. Hirschman, "The Turn to Authoritarianism in Latin America and the Search for Its Economic Determinants," pp. 73–74.

7. On how the removal of import controls and exchange restrictions, and a devaluation of the currency, create strong inflationary pressures, see Michael Wallerstein, "The Collapse of Democracy in Brazil," p. 29.

8. This argument is slightly different from the others in that the authoritarian regime is thought to be needed to repress not only the lower classes, but also a variety of other social groups, including the bourgeoisie. In assuming a greater autonomy of the military, this argument fits quite well the broader conjecture that military regimes emerged in the third world in order to increase the autonomy of their respective states, an autonomy which would be necessary to their development. For this argument see Irving L. Horowitz and Ellen K. Trimberger, "State Power and Military Nationalism in Latin America," *Comparative Politics* 8 (1976): 223–44; Ellen K. Trimberger, *Revolution from Above* (New Brunswick, N.J.: Transaction Books, 1978).

9. Samuel A. Morley and Gordon W. Smith, "The Effects of Changes in the Distribution of Income on Labor, Foreign Investment, and Growth in Brazil," in Alfred Stepan, ed., *Authoritarian Brazil* (New Haven: Yale University Press, 1973).

10. For data on the expenditure of workers, see José Serra, "Three Mistaken Theses Regarding the Connection between Industrialization

and Authoritarian Regimes," in David Collier, ed., *The New Authoritarianism in Latin America.*

11. See Albert O. Hirschman, "The Turn to Authoritarianism in Latin America and the Search for Its Economic Determinants," p. 81.

12. For ample evidence supporting this point, see José Serra, "Three Mistaken Theses Regarding the Connection between Industrialization and Authoritarian Regimes," pp. 117–27; Robert Kaufman, "Industrial Change and Authoritarian Rule in Latin America: A Concrete Review of the Bureaucratic-Authoritarian Model," in David Collier, ed., *The New Authoritarianism in Latin America,* pp. 165–254.

13. See José Serra, "Three Mistaken Theses Regarding the Connection between Industrialization and Authoritarian Regimes," pp. 127–28; A. O. Hirschman, "The Turn to Authoritarianism in Latin America and the Search for Its Economic Determinants," p. 76.

14. See Serra, "Three Mistaken Theses," pp.110–11; Hirschman, "The Turn to Authoritarianism," pp. 80–81.

15. Wallerstein draws on Fishlow's and Hirschman's conjectures on inflation, to argue that the slowdown of growth triggered high levels of inflation as a way to appease the severe social conflict that it generated. See Albert Fishlow, "Some Reflections on Post-1964 Brazilian Economic Policy," in Alfred Stepan, ed., *Authoritarian Brazil,* pp. 69–118; A. O. Hirschman, "The Social and Political Matrix of Inflation: Elaborations on the Latin American Experience," in A. O. Hirschman, *Essays in Trespassing: Economics to Politics and Beyond* (Cambridge: Cambridge University Press, 1980). For Wallerstein's argument, see Michael Wallerstein, "The Collapse of Democracy in Brazil."

16. Hirschman, "The Turn to Authoritarianism," p. 70.

17. Ibid., p. 79.

18. See chapter 2, pp. 9–22.

19. For a survey of the motives of the military in a wide variety of military coups, see Eric A. Nordlinger, *Soldiers in Politics: Military Coups and Governments* (Englewood Cliffs: Prentice-Hall, 1977).

20. Guillermo O'Donnell, *Modernization and Bureaucratic-Authoritarianism,* p. 69.

21. Ibid.

22. See notes 23, 24, and 25 below.

23. There are several reasons for which the military are reluctant to intervene. As students of the military in the third world have shown, most officers in those countries subscribe to the civilian ethic. These "legalist" officers believe in the principle of civilian supremacy, and will intervene only as a measure of last resort. Even if they believe a coup is warranted because the incumbent government is corrupt, incompetent, or subversive, or because it poses a threat to the corporate interests of the military, legalist officers are usually reluctant to intervene unless the

government's legitimacy among civilians has been seriously eroded. Officers are reluctant to intervene against a legitimate government not only for normative reasons. Intervening against a reasonably popular incumbent could mean governing in a highly turbulent environment. Civilians may organize protest movements that can cause much disorder, and splits within the military may follow. The military could therefore be thrust into the highly unpopular role of a police force and be unable to establish an efficient government, all of which would ultimately undermine the legitimacy of military institutions. For these points, see Eric Nordlinger, *Soldiers in Politics,* pp. 63–107; Alfred Stepan, *The Military in Politics,* pp. 189–90; Alfred Stepan, "Political Leadership and Regime Breakdown: Brazil," in Juan J. Linz and Alfred Stepan, eds., *The Breakdown of Democratic Regimes: Brazil* (Baltimore: Johns Hopkins University Press, 1978), pp. 121–22; John S. Fitch, *The Military Coup d'Etat as a Political Process: Ecuador, 1948–1966* (Baltimore: Johns Hopkins University Press, 1977), pp. 6–10.

24. For a detailed description of the basic reforms and the debates they generated, see Thomas Skidmore, *Politics in Brazil* (Oxford: Oxford University Press, 1967), chap. 7. For evidence showing there was a favorable climate for moderate reforms at the beginning of Goulart's term, see Argelina Figueiredo, "Political Coalitions in Brazil, 1961–1964: Alternatives to the Political Crisis," Ph.D. diss. (University of Chicago, 1987), chap. 4. On the position of workers and organized labor, see Timothy F. Harding, "The Political History of Organized Labor in Brazil," Ph.D. diss. (Stanford University, 1973), chaps. 9 and 10; Kenneth P. Erickson, *The Brazilian Corporative State and Working-Class Politics* (Berkeley: University of California Press, 1977); Youssef Cohen, *The Manipulation of Consent: The State and Working-Class Consciousness in Brazil* (Pittsburgh: University of Pittsburgh Press, 1989).

25. Paul Sigmund, *The Politics of Chile and the Overthrow of Allende* (Pittsburgh: University of Pittsburgh Press, 1977); Arturo Valenzuela, *The Breakdown of Democratic Regimes: Chile* (Baltimore: Johns Hopkins University Press, 1978).

26. Alfred Stepan, *The Military in Politics,* pp. 143–47; Alfred Stepan, "Political Leadership and Regime Breakdown: Brazil," pp. 115–19.

27. Alfred Stepan, *The Military in Politics,* p. 146.

28. Juan J. Linz, *The Breakdown of Democratic Regimes: Crisis, Breakdown, and Reequilibration* (Baltimore: Johns Hopkins University Press, 1979), esp. pp. 24–27; Arturo Valenzuela, *The Breakdown of Democratic Regimes: Chile;* Wanderley Guilherme dos Santos, "The Calculus of Conflict: Impasse in Brazilian Politics and the Crisis of 1964," Ph.D. diss. (Stanford University, 1979).

29. For the model of polarized pluralism, see Giovanni Sartori, "Eu-

ropean Political Parties: The Case of Polarized Pluralism," in Joseph LaPalombara and Myron Weiner, eds., *Political Parties and Political Development* (Princeton: Princeton University Press, 1966), pp. 137–76; Giovanni Sartori, *Parties and Party Systems: A Framework for Analysis* (Cambridge: Cambridge University Press, 1976), pp. 131–72.

30. Giovanni Sartori, *Parties and Party Systems,* p. 134.

31. Ibid., p. 140.

32. For what follows see Arturo Valenzuela, *The Breakdown of Democratic Regimes: Chile,* pp. xiii–xiv, 4–7.

33. Ibid., pp. 6–7.

34. On the Brazilian party system see Maria do Carmo Campello de Souza, *Estado e Partidos Politicos no Brasil* (São Paulo: Editora Alfa-Omega, 1976).

35. According to W. G. dos Santos, the political deadlock that eventually led to a military regime was caused not so much by a conservative reaction of Congress to the reforms; rather, a decisional paralysis was caused by the fragmentation and polarization of the party system. He shows that after Quadros's resignation, the party system moved toward a situation of polarized pluralism. See Wanderley Guilherme dos Santos, "The Calculus of Conflict: Impasse in Brazilian Politics and the Crisis of 1964," chaps. 1 and 2, n. 27.

36. Giovanni Sartori, *Parties and Party Systems,* pp. 140–45.

37. Wanderley Guilherme dos Santos, "Autoritarismo e Após: Convergências e Divergências entre Brasil e Chile," *Dados* 25 (1982): 151–63.

38. A few students of democratic breakdown have recognized the need for an incorporation of intentional phenomena in the explanation of democratic breakdown. Stepan, Valenzuela, and especially Figueiredo have come the closest to elaborating an intentional explanation of breakdown. Their historical accounts, however, fall short of providing a truly intentional explanation. They fail to capture the complex dynamic interaction among the actors involved in the process that led to the collapse of democratic institutions. This point will become obvious in the following chapters. See Alfred Stepan, "Political Leadership and Regime Breakdown: Brazil"; Arturo Valenzuela, *The Breakdown of Democratic Regimes: Chile;* Argelina Figueiredo, "Political Coalitions in Brazil, 1961–1964."

Chapter 4

1. Jon Elster, *Explaining Technical Change* (Cambridge: Cambridge University Press, 1983), p. 70 (emphasis supplied).

2. For a detailed discussion of these requirements, see Jon Elster, *Explaining Technical Change,* pp. 70–72; Jon Elster, "Introduction," in Jon

Elster, ed., *Rational Choice* (New York: New York University Press, 1986), pp. 12–16.

3. There is much controversy over the nature of the relationship between intention and action. On the one hand, "positivists"—those who are for the application of the methods of natural science in the social sciences—have argued that intentions can be seen as causes of action. According to this argument, one can therefore construct causal explanations (deductive-nomological explanations) of human action on the basis of human intentions (as the explanans). On the other hand, the "interpretivists"—those for whom the natural science methods do not apply to the study of human affairs—have argued that intention and action are internally related. According to them, intentions are an integral part of the definition of an action, which means that they cannot be the causes of action. Therefore, one cannot construct causal explanations of human action on the basis of intentions. In this book I borrow from Donald Davidson and Jon Elster, who argue that there is no reason either to believe that intentions cannot be causes of action or to believe that the positivist and interpretivist approaches are incompatible. See Donald Davidson, *Essays on Actions and Events* (New York: Oxford University Press, 1980), pp. 3–20, 149–62, 207–28, 245–76; Jon Elster, *Explaining Technical Change,* pp. 21–23. For the debate on this issue see Peter Winch, *The Idea of a Social Science and Its Relation to Philosophy* (London: Routledge and Kegan Paul, 1958); Peter Winch, "Understanding a Primitive Society," *American Philosophical Quarterly* 1 (1964): 307–24; G. E. M. Anscombe, *Intention* (Oxford: Basil Blackwell, 1957); W. H. Dray, *Laws and Explanation in History* (Oxford: Oxford University Press, 1957); G. H. Von Wright, *Explanation and Understanding* (Ithaca: Cornell University Press, 1971); Alasdair MacIntyre, "The Idea of a Social Science," in A. MacIntyre, *Against the Self-Images of the Age* (New York: Schocken, 1971); J. Donald Moon, "The Logic of Political Inquiry: A Synthesis of Opposed Perspectives," in Fred I. Greenstein and Nelson Polsby, eds., *Handbook of Political Science,* vol. 1 (Reading, Mass.: Addison-Wesley, 1975). See also the essays in F. R. Dallmayr and T. A. McCarthy, eds., *Understanding and Social Inquiry* (Notre Dame: University of Notre Dame Press, 1977), and P. Rabinow and W. M. Sullivan, eds., *Interpretive Social Science: A Reader* (Berkeley: University of California Press, 1979).

4. The example is from Donald Davidson, *Essays on Actions and Events,* p. 78. Quoted in Jon Elster, *Sour Grapes* (Cambridge: Cambridge University Press, 1983), p. 4.

5. Full details on consistency and other criteria for rational behavior are given below. See pp. 40–42.

6. This follows from two propositions in formal logic: (1) The conjunction of a proposition and its negation is a contradiction; (2) Any-

thing can follow from a false antecedent. From these two propositions one can infer that anything follows from contradictory beliefs. See George Tsebelis, *Nested Games: Rational Choice in Comparative Politics* (Berkeley: University of California Press, 1990), p. 25.

7. For greater detail on the relation between intentionality and rationality, see Jon Elster, *Explaining Technical Change,* pp. 72–73.

8. See Jon Elster, *Ulysses and the Sirens* (Cambridge: Cambridge University Press, 1979), chap. 4; Jon Elster, *Sour Grapes,* chap. 2.

9. Rationality is not the same as maximizing expected utility, for there are other decision rules that would qualify as rational. But the overwhelming majority of rational-choice studies adopt maximization of expected utility as the criterion for rationality. For some clear discussions of the rational-choice model of economic theory, as well as of some of its problems, see M. Friedman, "The Methodology of Positive Economics," in M. Friedman, *Essays in Positive Economics* (Chicago: University of Chicago Press, 1953); Gary Becker, *The Economic Approach to Human Behavior* (Chicago: University of Chicago Press, 1976); J. C. Harsanyi, "Rational-Choice Models of Political Behavior vs. Functionalist and Conformist Theories," *World Politics* 21 (1969): 513–38; J. C. Harsanyi, "Advances in Understanding Rational Behavior," in Jon Elster, ed., *Rational Choice,* pp. 82–107; A. K. Sen, "Choice Functions and Revealed Preferences," *Review of Economic Studies* 38 (1971); "Behavior and the Concept of Preference," in J. Elster, ed., *Rational Choice,* pp. 60–81; Donald Davidson, *Essays on Actions and Events.*

10. For a fuller discussion of the axioms an actor's behavior must satisfy in order to be the kind of behavior involved in maximizing one's expected utility, see R. D. Luce and H. Raiffa, *Games and Decisions* (New York: Wiley, 1957); W. H. Riker and P. C. Ordeshook, *An Introduction to Positive Political Theory* (Englewood Cliffs: Prentice-Hall, 1973); P. C. Ordeshook, *Game Theory and Political Theory: An Introduction* (Cambridge: Cambridge University Press, 1986); Martin Shubik, *Game Theory in the Social Sciences: Concepts and Solutions* (Cambridge: MIT Press, 1984).

11. For a clear, concise statement of what this requirement entails, see George Tsebelis, *Nested Games: Rational Choice in Comparative Politics,* pp. 26–27.

12. For an exhaustive discussion of the "thin" and "broad" theories of rationality, see Jon Elster, *Sour Grapes,* chap. 1.

13. For the notions of rational beliefs and rational desires, see Jon Elster, *Ulysses and the Sirens,* pp. 157–79; *Sour Grapes,* pp. 15–26; *Rational Choice,* pp. 17–22.

14. While it may make sense to speak abstractly of beliefs that are "plausible given the evidence," it is in practice very difficult to say that a particular belief meets this requirement. For some suggestions as to

how this can be done, see Jon Elster, *Sour Grapes,* pp. 16–18; *Rational Choice,* p. 14.

15. The literature on irrational belief-formation is very large. Some well-known works are: Donald Davidson, "Paradoxes of Irrationality," in R. Wolheim and J. Hopkins, eds., *Philosophical Essays on Freud* (Cambridge: Cambridge University Press, 1982); Donald Davidson, *Essays on Actions and Events,* esp. pp. 21–42; David Pears, *Motivated Irrationality* (Oxford: Oxford University Press, 1984); Jon Elster, *Ulysses and the Sirens; Sour Grapes;* Alfred R. Mele, *Irrationality: An Essay on Akrasia, Self-Deception, and Self-Control* (Oxford: Oxford University Press, 1987); Robert Dunn, *The Possibility of Weakness of Will* (Indianapolis: Hackett, 1987); William Charlton, *Weakness of Will: A Philosophical Introduction* (New York: Basil Blackwell, 1988); H. Fingarette, *Self-Deception* (London: Routledge and Kegan Paul, 1969).

16. The example is from William Charlton, *Weakness of Will,* p. 141.

17. In recent years, attribution theorists have argued that much of the irrational behavior that was once explained by motivational theories such as dissonance theory can be explained by purely cognitive factors. Attribution theorists have gone so far as to argue that even ethnic prejudice can be explained by purely "cold," nonmotivational mechanisms. See Richard Nisbett and Lee Ross, *Human Inference: Strategies and Shortcomings of Social Judgement* (Englewood Cliffs: Prentice-Hall, 1980), pp. 237–42. For other empirical studies challenging dissonance theory and motivational hypotheses, see D. Bem, "An Experimental Analysis of Self-Persuasion," *Journal of Experimental Social Psychology* 1 (1965): 199–218; D. Bem, "Self-Perception: An Alternative Interpretation of Cognitive Dissonance Phenomena," *Psychological Review* 74 (1967): 183–200; D. Bem, "Self-Perception Theory," *Advances in Experimental Social Psychology* 6 (1972): 1–62; D. Miller and M. Ross, "Self-Serving Biases in the Attribution of Causality: Fact or Fiction?" *Psychological Bulletin* 82 (1975): 213–35. These and other studies have prompted a vigorous debate between attribution theorists and defenders of motivational hypotheses. For this debate, see J. Harvey and G. Weary, "Current Issues in Attribution Theory and Research," *Annual Review of Psychology* 35 (1984): 427–59.

18. There is nothing wrong with using the evidence most available to memory or perception to make inferences and predictions about the likelihood of certain events. But one should always be alert to the possible biases of personal experience and of current data, and experiments show that usually people are not. On the misuse of "available" data (or of the "availability heuristic") see Richard Nisbett and Lee Ross, *Human Inference: Strategies and Shortcomings of Social Judgement;* D. Kahneman, P. Slovic, and A. Tversky, eds., *Judgement under Uncertainty*

(Cambridge: Cambridge University Press, 1982). These works also show that people misuse simplifying "knowledge structures"—theories, images, scripts, schema—that are otherwise useful to process information. Experiments show that people tend to ignore or distort information that does not fit their knowledge structures. Ignorance about statistical inference is another major source of error. People consistently make mistakes involving inferences from samples to populations, make erroneous judgments about covariation and causality, and have little knowledge of the regression considerations underlying prediction. Humans also have trouble understanding the notion of randomness; they underestimate the amount of clustering in random processes. For example, Londoners erroneously inferred an intentional pattern in German bombing from their observation that bombs fell in clusters during the blitz. See Nisbett and Ross, *Human Inference,* chaps. 4–8. For the example just mentioned see Jon Elster, *Nuts and Bolts for the Social Sciences* (Cambridge: Cambridge University Press, 1989), p. 39.

19. For this and other examples of the misuse of the "availability heuristic," see R. Nisbett and L. Ross, *Human Inference,* pp. 56–57.

20. For a full discussion of this difficult topic, see Jon Elster, *Sour Grapes,* especially chap. 3.

21. By the same token, people might overvalue what they can get. The opposite phenomenon—counteradaptive preference formation—is far more perverse, and harder to fathom. It consists in preferring what one cannot get: the grass is always greener on the other side of the fence.

22. For some of the rational-choice theorists who advocate an approach that is both individualist and structuralist, see M. Taylor, ed., *Rationality and Revolution* (Cambridge: Cambridge University Press, 1988); Robert H. Bates, *Essays on the Political Economy of Rural Africa* (Berkeley: University of California Press, 1987); Margaret Levi, *Of Rule and Revenue* (Berkeley: University of California Press, 1988); Douglass C. North, *Structure and Change in Economic History* (New York: Norton, 1981). For one of the rare uses of such a rational-choice approach in the study of Latin American politics, see Barbara Geddes, "A Game Theoretic Model of Reform in Latin American Democracies," *American Political Science Review* 85 (June 1991): 371–92.

23. For this distinction, see Jon Elster, *Explaining Technical Change,* pp. 74–83; *Rational Choice, pp. 7–8.*

24. However, this does not mean that an equilibrium point will always exist. There are various situations in which no equilibrium exists and other situations in which more than one equilibrium point exists. For a concise discussion of those situations, see Jon Elster, *Ulysses and the Sirens,* chap. 3; Jon Elster, *Rational Choice,* pp. 17–22.

25. For a fuller treatment of what follows, see David M. Kreps, *A Course in Microeconomic Theory* (Princeton: Princeton University

Press, 1990); Martin Shubik, *Game Theory in the Social Sciences: Concepts and Solutions* (Cambridge: MIT Press, 1984); Roger B. Meyerson, *Game Theory: Analysis of Conflict* (Cambridge: Harvard University Press, 1991); Ken Binmore, *Fun and Games* (Lexington, Mass.: D. C. Heath, 1992); James Friedman, *Game Theory with Applications to Economics* (Cambridge: MIT Press, 1990); Eric Rasmussen, *Games and Information* (New York: Blackwell, 1989); D. Fundenberg and J. Tirole, *Game Theory* (Cambridge: MIT Press, 1991); P. C. Ordeshook, *Game Theory and Political Theory* (Cambridge: Cambridge University Press, 1986); Steven J. Brams, *Game Theory and Politics* (New York: Free Press, 1975); Steven J. Brams, *Paradoxes in Politics* (New York: Free Press, 1976).

26. The literature on the prisoner's dilemma is enormous. For references see the bibliographies in the books mentioned in note 25. For some studies of the prisoner's dilemma in connection with political phenomena and problems, see Mancur Olson, *The Logic of Collective Action* (Cambridge: Harvard University Press, 1968); Michael Taylor, *Anarchy and Cooperation* (London: John Wiley, 1976); Michael Taylor, *The Possibility of Cooperation* (Cambridge: Cambridge University Press, 1976); Russell Hardin, *Collective Action* (Baltimore: Johns Hopkins University Press, 1982); Robert Axelrod, *The Evolution of Cooperation* (New York: Basic Books, 1984).

27. Robert Axelrod, *The Evolution of Cooperation,* p. 9

28. Ibid., p. 7.

29. Friedman proved the existence of multiple equilibria in iterated games. See J. Friedman, "A Noncooperative Equilibrium for Supergames," *Review of Economic Studies* 38 (1971): 1–12.

30. George Tsebelis, *Nested Games,* p. 73.

31. For what follows, see ibid., pp. 74–75.

32. Robert Axelrod, *The Evolution of Cooperation,* p. 11.

33. See George Tsebelis, *Nested Games,* p. 74. For the rather restrictive conditions under which the cooperative strategy outlined by Axelrod can emerge, see Michael Taylor, *The Possibility of Cooperation.*

34. George Tsebelis, *Nested Games,* p. 74.

35. D. Fudenberg and E. Maskin, "The Folk Theorem in Repeated Games with Discounting or with Incomplete Information," *Econometrica* 54 (1986): 533–54.

36. For a recent interesting discussion on the problems posed by the fact that iterated games have an infinite number of equilibria, see Michael Hechter, "Comment: On the Inadequacy of Game Theory for the Solution of Real-World Collective Action Problems," in Karen S. Cook and Margaret Levi, eds., *The Limits of Rationality* (Chicago: University of Chicago Press, 1990).

37. George Tsebelis, *Nested Games,* pp. 77–78.

Chapter 5

1. What follows is a brief summary of the general structural explanation of the breakdown of democracy in Latin America. It stresses the features shared by all such structural explanations. For the specific variations and their problems, see the discussion in chapter 3 of this book.

2. Hirschman has made it difficult not to have doubts about such "impossibilities." He has convincingly argued that there was much more room for economic expansion after the easy phase of import-substituting industrialization than the structuralists have suggested, and that the "either major structural change or doom" theories might have served well the psychic needs of their formulators but were detrimental to the very economies they purported to heal. To the extent that this is the case, the structuralist case that only an authoritarian regime could have maintained capitalism without major structural reforms clearly does not hold much water. See A. O. Hirschman, "The Political Economy of Import-Substituting Industrialization in Latin America," in A. O. Hirschman, *A Bias for Hope* (New Haven: Yale University Press, 1971), pp. 85–123; A. O. Hirschman, "The Turn to Authoritarianism in Latin America and the Search for Its Economic Determinants," in David Collier, *The New Authoritarianism in Latin America* (Princeton: Princeton University Press, 1979), pp. 61–98.

3. See chapter 2. Of special relevance are the papers by Robert Kaufman, "Industrial Change and Authoritarian Rule in Latin America: A Concrete Review of the Bureaucratic-Authoritarian Model," in David Collier, ed., *The New Authoritarianism in Latin America,* pp. 165–254, and José Serra, "Three Mistaken Theses Regarding the Connection between Industrialization and Authoritarian Regimes," in David Collier, ed., *The New Authoritarianism in Latin America,* pp. 99–164.

4. For some discussions of the issues concerning reforms in Brazil in the sixties, see Thomas E. Skidmore, *Politics in Brazil* (New York: Oxford University Press, 1967), esp. pp. 234–48; Alfred Stepan, "Political Leadership and Regime Breakdown: Brazil," in Juan Linz and Alfred Stepan, eds., *The Breakdown of Democratic Regimes* (Baltimore: Johns Hopkins University Press, 1978), pp. 110–37; Argelina M. C. Figueiredo, "Political Coalitions in Brazil, 1961–1964: Alternatives to the Political Crisis," Ph.D. diss. (University of Chicago, 1987); Moniz Bandeira, *O Governo João Goulart: As Lutas Sociais no Brazil* (Rio: Civilização Brasileira, 1977); Aspásia Camargo, "A Questão Agrária: Crise de Poder e Reformas de Base (1930–1964)," in *História Geral da Civilização Brasileira,* Tomo III, vol. 3 (São Paulo: Difel, 1977), pp. 121–224.

5. For the program of agrarian reform of the Frei administration, see Jeannine Swift, *Agrarian Reform in Chile* (Lexington: D. C. Heath, 1971); Robert R. Kaufman, *The Politics of Land Reform in Chile* (Cambridge: Harvard University Press, 1972); Paul E. Sigmund, *The Over-*

throw of Allende and the Politics of Chile, 1964–1976 (Pittsburgh: University of Pittsburgh Press, 1977); Stefan De Vylder, *Allende's Chile: The Political Economy of the Rise and Fall of the Unidad Popular* (Cambridge: Cambridge University Press, 1976).

6. For evidence on the amount and sources of support for Goulart and his basic reforms, see Argelina M. C. Figueiredo, "Political Coalitions in Brazil, 1961–1964," chap. 4.

7. See chapter 3, pp. 33–36.

8. On the debates and negotiations concerning agrarian reform in Brazil, see Aspásia de Alcantara Camargo, "A Questão Agrária: Crise de Poder e Reformas de Base (1930–1964)," pp. 188–222; Argelina M. C. Figueiredo, "Political Coalitions in Brazil, 1961–1964," especially chap. 4

9. This was the case in both of the situations studied in the next two chapters. See Argelina M. C. Figueiredo, "Political Coalitions in Brazil, 1961–1964"; Arturo Valenzuela, *The Breakdown of Democratic Regimes: Chile* (Baltimore: Johns Hopkins University Press, 1978). For further details, see chapters 6 and 7 of this book.

10. See chapter 3, note 23.

Elsewhere I have shown how the right in Brazil maneuvered to split the coalition of moderates so as to gain sufficient civilian support for a military coup in 1964. See Youssef Cohen, "The Heresthetics of Coup Making," *Comparative Political Studies* 24 (October 1991): 344–64; Youssef Cohen, "Democracy from Above: The Political Origins of Military Dictatorship in Brazil," *World Politics* 40 (1987): 30–54.

11. See note 9 above.

Chapter 6

1. On the Brazilian democratic period of 1945–64, see Thomas E. Skidmore, *Politics in Brazil, 1930–1964: An Experiment in Democracy* (New York: Oxford University Press, 1967); Peter Flynn, *Brazil: A Political Analysis* (Boulder: Westview Press, 1983). For studies on the structure of the political system during that period, see Gláucio A. D. Soares, *Sociedade e Política no Brasil* (São Paulo: Difel, 1973); Maria do Carmo C. de Souza, *Estado e Partidos Políticos no Brasil* (São Paulo: Alfa-Õmega, 1976); Simon Schwartzman, *São Paulo e o Estado Nacional* (São Paulo: Difel, 1975); Francisco Weffort, *O Populismo na Política Brasileira* (São Paulo: Paz e Terra, 1980); Barry Ames, *Political Survival: Politicians and Public Policy in Latin America* (Berkeley: University of California Press, 1987); Wanderley Guilherme dos Santos, "The Calculus of Conflict: Impasse in Brazilian Politics and the Crisis of 1964," Ph.D. diss. (Stanford University, 1979).

2. On the resignation of Jânio Quadros and the political crisis it triggered, see Thomas Skidmore, *Politics in Brazil,* chap. 6; Wanderley G.

dos Santos, "The Calculus of Conflict," especially chaps. 3 and 4; Argelina M. C. Figueiredo, "Political Coalitions in Brazil, 1961–1964: Democratic Alternatives to the Political Crisis," Ph.D. diss. (University of Chicago, 1987), chap. 2.

3. The attempted coup of 1961, to prevent Goulart from succeeding Quadros, was led by the three military ministers of Quadros's government. It failed mainly because high-ranking officers were divided on the issue of Goulart's accession to the presidency. For an analysis of this attempted coup, see Alfred Stepan, *The Military in Politics* (Princeton: Princeton University Press, 1971), chap. 5.

4. Goulart was a cattle-breeder from Rio Grande do Sul, whose family was part of the power network of the Vargas clan in the Riograndense municipio of São Borja. Far from being a radical, he was a member of the established elite who exploited Vargas's "trabalhismo" for his own political purposes. Nevertheless, Goulart did much to strengthen leftist politicians and militant labor leaders, and he played a major role in giving major reforms a priority on the national agenda. On Goulart's career, and his ties to the left, see Thomas Skidmore, *Politics in Brazil;* Kenneth P. Erickson, *The Brazilian Corporative State and Working-Class Politics* (Berkeley: University of California Press, 1977), especially chaps. 5, 6, and 7; Moniz Bandeira, *O Govêrno João Goulart: As Lutas Sociais no Brasil (1961–1964)* (Rio de Janeiro: Civilização Brasileira, 1983); Caio N. Toledo, *O Govêrno Goulart e o Golpe de 64* (São Paulo: Brasiliense, 1982). On the PTB, and Goulart's relationship with the PTB, see Lucilia de Almeida Neves Delgado, *PTB: Do Getulismo ao Reformismo (1945–1964)* (São Paulo: Marco Zero, 1989); Maria Celina Soares D'Araujo, *O Segundo Govêrno Vargas, 1950–1954* (Rio de Janeiro: Zahar, 1982); Maria Victoria Benevides, *O PTB e o Trabalhismo: Partido e Sindicato em São Paulo, 1945–1964* (São Paulo: Brasiliense, 1989).

5. For the conflict over Goulart's accession to the presidency, and the composition and motivations of the groups favoring Goulart's accession, see Alfred Stepan, *The Military in Politics,* chap. 5; Thomas Skidmore, *Politics in Brazil,* pp. 205–15; A. Labaki, *1961: A Crise da Renúncia e a Solução Parlamentarista* (São Paulo: Brasiliense, 1986).

6. Goulart's "basic reforms" included administrative, financial, educational, agrarian, and tax reforms. His program also included extending the vote to illiterates and the granting of political rights to enlisted military men, as well as the legalization of the Communist Party. See Thomas Skidmore, *Politics in Brazil,* pp. 234–38; Moniz Bandeira, *O Govêrno João Goulart,* especially chaps. 4 and 13. For a discussion of the parliamentary system, and how it could have slowed down the implementation of reforms, see Argelina Figueiredo, "Political Coalitions in Brazil," chap. 3.

7. Under a parliamentary system the powers of the president were to be greatly limited. The constitutional amendment that instituted the parliamentary regime gave the prime minister many of the privileges formerly held by the president. Only the prime minister could propose bills as well as the government budget, and only he could decree and execute federal intervention as well as a state of siege. And all acts of the president would have to be countersigned by the prime minister and the heads of the relevant ministries. Although the amendment still gave the president the right to dissolve Congress and call new elections, it ruled that this provision would apply only to the following legislature. This meant that Goulart was in fact barred from using this prerogative to attempt to form a new congress that would be more favorable to radical reforms. In addition, the military opposed to Goulart saw to it that a clause concerning national security, under which the president could be impeached, was included in the constitutional act instituting the parliamentary regime. All of this meant that Goulart would have much greater difficulty in implementing a sweeping program of reforms in a relatively short period of time. See Argelina Figueiredo, "Political Coalitions in Brazil," chap. 3.

8. On the PSD and its position toward reforms, see Lúcia Hippólito, *De Rapôsas e Reformistas: O PSD e a Experiência Democrática Brasileira (1945–1964)* (Rio de Janeiro: Paz e Terra, 1985), especially chap. 8.

9. For details on the opposition to parliamentarism, see Thomas Skidmore, *Politics in Brazil,* pp. 211–23; Argelina Figueiredo, "Political Coalitions in Brazil," chap. 3.

10. Some influential politicians from the PSD, like Juscelino Kubitscheck, who was the presidential candidate most likely to win in 1965, went so far as to vote against the Additional Act that instituted the parliamentary regime. Kubitscheck then became one of the major leaders of the campaign for a return to presidentialism. See Thomas Skidmore, *Politics in Brazil,* p. 221; Lúcia Hippólito, *De Rapôsas e Reformistas,* pp. 215–23.

11. See Thomas Skidmore, *Politics in Brazil,* p. 223.

12. Two major proponents of this thesis are Celso Furtado, "Political Obstacles to the Economic Development of Brazil," in Claudio Veliz, ed., *Obstacles to Change in Latin America* (London: Oxford University Press, 1965), and Hélio Jaguaribe, *Condições Institucionais do Desenvolvimento Brasileiro* (Rio de Janeiro: ISEB, 1958). For a theoretical and empirical critique of this thesis, see Wanderley G. dos Santos, *The Calculus of Conflict.*

13. *Correio da Manhã,* April 27, 1963. Quoted in Argelina Figueiredo, "Political Coalitions in Brazil," p. 149. For more evidence on the willingness of the majority of moderates, even among the most con-

servative parties, to enact land reform, see Carlos Castelo Branco, *Introdução à Revolução de 1964,* vol. 1 (Rio de Janeiro: Artenova, 1975), pp. 150, 158, 189.

14. For the distribution of seats in the Chamber of Deputies and in the Senate, from 1945 to 1962, see Lúcia Hippólito, *De Rapôsas e Reformistas,* pp. 57–58.

15. See ibid.

16. Most of the PSD politicians were reacting pragmatically to the changing times. As the leading party, and the party of the center, the PSD missed the opportunity to assume the direction of the inevitable march toward social reforms. This is what the younger generation of the mid-fifties wanted the party to do. But the older politicians defeated the young turks—the so-called "ala moça" of the PSD—to the great loss of the party. For an account of the trajectory of the PSD in the fifties and sixties, see Lúcia Hippólito, *De Rapôsas e Reformistas,* chaps. 6, 7, and 8.

17. On the tensions between landowner associations and the PSD where agrarian reform was concerned, see Aspasia de Alcantara Camargo, "A Questão Agrária: Crise de Poder e Reformas de Base (1930–1964)," in *História Geral da Civilização Brasileira,* Tomo III, vol. 3 (São Paulo: Difel, 1977), pp. 212–17.

18. For the full text of the Declaration of Brasilia see Lúcia Hippólito, *De Rapôsas e Reformistas,* pp. 309–16.

19. The "Bossa Nova" was formed in opposition to Lacerda and the "Banda de Musica." The group defined itself as being of the "center-left," and it supported a program of economic development with social justice—a program of Christian inspiration much like that of the Chilean Christian Democrats. Formed by politicians like José Sarney, José Aparecido, and Clovis Ferro Costa, the "Bossa Nova" wanted to impart a far more progressive direction to the UDN. See Maria Victoria de Mesquita Benevides, *A UDN e o Udenismo: Ambiguidades do Liberalismo Brasileiro (1945–1965)* (Rio de Janeiro: Paz e Terra, 1981), pp. 113–25, 189–96.

20. In its "Carta de Principios" of 1962, the UDN had explicitly supported the payment of expropriated land in public bonds and the constitutional amendment such payment required as well. The UDN maintained this position until April of 1963, when it decided to oppose any constitutional amendment proposed by Goulart and the PTB. See ibid., pp. 190–93.

21. During the National Convention of the UDN that took place in Curitiba in April of 1963, the right-wingers led by Carlos Lacerda, Herbert Levy, and Ernani Satiro persuaded the apprehensive majority of UDN politicians to oppose any constitutional amendment proposed by

Goulart and the PTB. To a large extent, this change of heart was due to the fact that Goulart and the PTB had clearly included the demands of the radical left in their proposal for a constitutional amendment on agrarian reform. See Maria V. de Mesquita Benevides, *A UDN e o Udenismo,* pp. 189–96; Aspásia de A. Camargo, "A Questão Agrária," pp. 214–17; Argelina Figueiredo, "Political Coalitions in Brazil," pp. 134–37.

22. See note 14.

23. For details on the disagreements between the two parties, see Aspásia Camargo, "A Questão Agrária," pp. 208–17; Argelina Figueiredo, "Political Coalitions in Brazil," pp. 128–52. A fuller discussion can be found on pp. 88–89 of this book.

24. See pp. 88–89 of this book.

25. See note 4.

26. See notes 16 through 18 above.

27. For details on the several groups of extremists of both the left and the right, see Thomas Skidmore, *Politics in Brazil,* pp. 223–28, 276–84.

28. For ample evidence of the fear the PSD and the UDN had that the agrarian reform might be the first step toward the imposition of "communism" in Brazil under a dictatorship headed by Goulart, see Maria Benevides, *A UDN e o Udenismo no Brasil,* pp. 189–95; Lúcia Hippólito, *De Rapôsas e Reformistas,* pp. 213–42; Wanderley G. dos Santos, "The Calculus of Conflict," especially chap. 6. For Goulart's fears concerning the PSD and the UDN, see Thomas Skidmore, *Politics in Brazil,* chaps. 7 and 8; Kenneth P. Erickson, *The Brazilian Corporative State and Working-Class Politics,* chaps. 6 and 7, pp. 147–50; Wanderley G. dos Santos, "The Calculus of Conflict," pp. 192–93.

29. See notes 4 and 6 above.

30. For studies of the radical leftists, their organizations, their power within the labor movement, and their influence in postwar Brazilian politics, see Kenneth P. Erickson, *The Brazilian Corporative State and Working-Class Politics;* Timothy F. Harding, "The Political History of Organized Labor in Brazil," Ph.D. diss. (Stanford University, 1973), especially chaps. 9 and 10; Ronald H. Chilcote, *The Brazilian Communist Party: Conflict and Integration, 1922–1972* (New York: Oxford University Press, 1974); Lucilia de Almeida Neves Delgado, *O Comando Geral dos Trabalhadores, 1961–1964* (Petrópolis: Vozes, 1986); Leôncio M. Rodrigues, "O PCB: Os Dirigentes e a Organização," in *História Geral da Civilização Brasileira,* Tomo III, vol. 3 (São Paulo: Difel, 1977), pp. 361–433; Moisés Vinhas, *O Partidão: A Luta por um Partido de Massas, 1922–1974* (São Paulo: Hucitec, 1982); Sérgio A. Costa, *O CGT e as Lutas Sindicais Brasileiras (1960–1964)* (São Paulo: Grêmio Politecnico, 1981); Elide R. Bastos, *As Ligas Camponêsas* (Petrópolis:

Vozes, 1984); Edgar Carone, *O P.C.B. (1943–1964)* (São Paulo: Difel, 1982).

31. For a detailed study of the symbiotic relationship between Goulart and radical leftists, see Kenneth P. Erickson, *The Brazilian Corporative State and Working-Class Politics,* chaps. 5, 6, and 7. Also relevant are studies of the corporative labor structure, which show how politicians used it to mobilize working-class support. For some of these studies, see Leôncio Martins Rodrigues, *Conflito Industrial e Sindicalismo no Brasil* (São Paulo: Difel, 1966); José A. Rodrigues, *Sindicato e Desenvolvimento no Brasil* (São Paulo: Difel, 1968); Francisco Weffort, *O Populismo na Política Brasileira;* Luiz W. Vianna, *Liberalismo e Sindicato no Brasil* (Rio: Paz e Terra, 1976); Amaury de Souza, "The Nature of Corporative Representation: Leaders and Members of Organized Labor in Brazil," Ph.D. diss. (Massachusetts Institute of Technology, 1978); Kenneth S. Mericle, "Conflict Regulation in the Brazilian Industrial Relations System," Ph.D. diss. (University of Wisconsin, 1974); Philippe C. Schmitter, *Interest Conflict and Political Change in Brasil* (Stanford: Stanford University Press, 1968).

32. See note 28 above.

33. Enfranchising illiterates was part of Goulart's and the left's program of "basic reforms"; changing reelection rules was not. Yet Goulart pursued the latter as doggedly as he campaigned for reforms, thus reinforcing suspicions of "ulterior motives," of a hidden agenda, behind his rhetoric of change in the name of social justice.

34. Goulart's attempts occurred during the parliamentary years of his tenure, in 1961 and 1962. See Argelina Figueiredo, "Political Coalitions in Brazil," pp. 46, 73–74.

35. Goulart knew this, but could not cut his ties to the radicals. Instead, he vacillated between the center and the left, alternating concessions to the left with concessions to the center, which did not, of course, have the effects he wished it would have. See Thomas Skidmore, *Politics in Brazil,* chaps. 7 and 8, esp. pp. 244–52, 260–63, 266–67.

36. See ibid., p. 249.

37. Ibid.

38. See Moniz Bandeira, *O Governo João Goulart,* pp. 104–6.

39. For the political maneuvers of the more conservative members of the PSD, especially of its politicians from Minas Gerais, see Lúcia Hippólito, *De Rapôsas e Reformistas,* chap. 8.

40. See Thomas Skidmore, *Politics in Brazil,* p. 267.

41. Wanderley G. dos Santos, "The Calculus of Conflict," p. 192. See also Kenneth P. Erickson, *The Corporative State and Working-Class Politics,* p. 148.

42. In the end, this is exactly what the PSD did—it withdrew its support for a constitutional amendment and joined the UDN in a grand

coalition to veto any reform involving constitutional change. See Wanderley G. dos Santos, "The Calculus of Conflict," pp. 94–97, 190–93, 232–33.

43. This was Goulart's greatest fear. For evidence of this see references mentioned in notes 28 and 41.

44. Stepan has shown that the Brazilian military never intervened without substantial support from civilians. See Alfred Stepan, *The Military in Politics,* chap. 5. This is also true of other Latin American and third world countries. See Eric Nordlinger, *Soldiers in Politics: Military Coups and Governments* (Englewood Cliffs: Prentice-Hall, 1977), pp. 63–107.

45. This was the strategy adopted by the radical left, which Goulart and the PTB finally made their own in 1964. By then all of them were convinced that the bulk of the population would support them against the civilian-military coalition that wanted to depose Goulart. See Argelina Figueiredo, "Political Coalitions in Brazil," chap. 8; Thomas Skidmore, *Politics in Brazil,* pp. 276–302.

46. On the left's overestimation, see Thomas Skidmore, *Politics in Brazil,* pp. 276–84; Argelina Figueiredo, "Political Coalitions in Brazil," pp. 245–47; Kenneth P. Erickson, *The Corporative State and Working-Class Politics,* p. 122; Paulo R. Schilling, *Como se Coloca a Direita no Poder,* vol. 1 (São Paulo: Global, 1979), p. 233. For a fuller discussion, see the concluding pages of this chapter.

47. On the relations between Goulart and the PSD, see Lúcia Hippólito, *De Rapôsas e Reformistas,* pp. 232–47. For the links between the PSD and the UDN, see notes 28 and 39.

48. This is the line the younger generation of the PSD—the ala moça—wanted its party to adopt. But the older generation suppressed the younger voice of the party, preferring the more cautious strategy of maintaining a safe distance from Goulart and of only passively supporting a piecemeal program of reforms. See note 16 above.

49. See note 28 above.

50. Unlike the UDN, the PSD leadership had always tried to avoid military intervention. But there is no question that, if confronted with the possibility of a seizure of power by the left, it would join forces with the UDN and the military. On this point, see Lúcia Hippólito, *De Rapôsas e Reformistas,* chaps. 7 and 8.

51. What follows is based on Aspasia Camargo, *A Questão Agrária,* pp. 188–216; Moniz Bandeira, *O Governo João Goulart,* chaps. 4 and 13; Argelina Figueiredo, "Political Coalitions in Brazil," pp. 128–52; Wanderley G. dos Santos, "The Calculus of Conflict," pp. 186–236.

52. The politicians of the PSD felt that the inclusion of urban property in the amendment gave the government too much latitude to interfere with private property. See Argelina Figueiredo, "Political Coalitions

in Brazil," pp. 132–34; Lúcia Hippólito, *De Rapôsas e Reformistas,* pp. 230–31.

53. The testimony of Sérgio Magalhaes, a well-known representative of the PTB, says it all: "In spite of being a conservative party, the PSD was more open (than the UDN). The PSD had reached the point where it accepted a change in the Constitution, but we had an exalted faction which was never satisfied; so they also included an urban reform. In addition to the agrarian reform that was not yet achieved, they also wanted an urban reform. The PSD then backed out and joined the UDN." Quoted in Lúcia Hippólito, *De Rapôsas e Reformistas,* p. 231.

54. For the strategy and tactics of the extremists of both the left and the right, see Thomas Skidmore, *Politics in Brazil,* pp. 248–52, 260–67; Argelina Figueiredo, "Political Coalitions in Brazil," pp. 136–37, 147–50.

55. For an account of the breakdown of the negotiations, see Argelina Figueiredo, "Political Coalitions in Brazil," pp. 133–46.

56. See note 42 above.

57. See Argelina Figueiredo, "Political Coalitions in Brazil," p. 147.

58. Ibid., p. 148.

59. See note 54 above.

60. For details on the plan and its fate, see Thomas Skidmore, *Politics in Brazil,* pp. 234–59; Argelina Figueiredo, "Political Coalitions in Brazil," pp. 92–128. See also Robert T. Daland, *Brazilian Planning: Development Politics and Administration* (Chapel Hill: University of North Carolina Press, 1967); Lucilia de Almeida Neves Delgado, *CGT, 1961–1964.*

61. See Youssef Cohen, "Democracy from Above: The Political Origins of Military Dictatorship in Brazil," *World Politics* 40 (1987): 30–54; Argelina Figueiredo, "Political Coalitions in Brazil," pp. 97–128.

62. On the AMFORP issue, see Moniz Bandeira, *O Govêrno João Goulart,* chap. 8; Thomas Skidmore, *Politics in Brazil,* pp. 245–46.

63. The most notorious case of expropriation had been that of a subsidiary of the International Telephone and Telegraph Company, which was expropriated in February 1962 by Brizola, then governor of Rio Grande do Sul.

64. Thomas Skidmore, *Politics in Brazil,* p. 249.

65. See note 21 above.

66. For an account of this rebellion, see Thomas Skidmore, *Politics in Brazil,* pp. 260–61.

67. The military stated that they would intervene only if Goulart overstepped the boundaries of constitutionality. Their main motive was to stop Goulart and the left from overturning the democratic regime—as the central document of the anti-Goulart conspiracy, the memorandum circulated by Castelo Branco on March 20, 1964, would make clear. See

Thomas Skidmore, *Politics in Brazil,* p. 295. For greater detail on the motives of the conspirators and the evolution of the conspiracy, see René A. Dreifuss, *1964: A Conquista do Estado* (Petrópolis: Vozes, 1981). See also Ronald M. Schneider, *The Political System of Brazil: Emergence of a Modernizing Authoritarian Regime* (New York: Columbia University Press, 1971); Luiz V. Filho, *O Govêrno Castelo Branco* (Rio: José Olympio, 1975); Peter J. McDonough, *Power and Ideology in Brazil* (Princeton: Princeton University Press, 1981).

68. See Thomas Skidmore, *Politics in Brazil,* p. 261.

69. For a detailed account of Goulart's attempts to declare a state of siege and its effects, see Argelina Figueiredo, "Political Coalitions in Brazil," chap. 5.

70. For details on the SUPRA decree see Aspásia Camargo, *A Questão Agrária,* pp. 217–22.

71. On the Progressive Front, and the reasons for its failure, see Argelina Figueiredo, "Political Coalitions in Brazil," chap. 6; Thomas Skidmore, *Politics in Brazil,* pp. 278–89.

72. For a concise account of Goulart's final change in strategy in mid-March of 1964, see Alfred Stepan, "Political Leadership and Regime Breakdown: Brazil," in Juan J. Linz and Alfred Stepan, eds., *The Breakdown of Democratic Regimes: Latin America* (Baltimore: Johns Hopkins University Press, 1978), pp. 121–22.

73. Lúcia Hippólito, *De Rapôsas e Reformistas,* p. 242.

74. When the naval minister tried to quell the mutiny, Goulart dismissed him and allowed the labor leadership, which was clearly associated with the Communist Party, to participate in the choice of a new minister. This was too much even for the nationalist supporters of Goulart within the army. See Alfred Stepan, "Political Leadership and Regime Breakdown," pp. 130–31.

75. For evidence on Goulart's and the left's overestimation of their own power, see note 46.

76. The radical left had attempted to transform the corporative system from above, by gaining control of the top positions within the corporative labor structure rather than by directly organizing their mass base. See Kenneth P. Erickson, *The Corporative State and Working-Class Politics,* pp. 115–22; John Humphrey, *Capitalist Control and Workers' Struggle in the Brazilian Auto Industry* (Princeton: Princeton University Press, 1982).

77. Kenneth P. Erickson, *The Corporative State and Working-Class Politics,* p. 101.

Chapter 7

1. For Allende's and the Popular Unity's program see Stefan de Vylder, *Allende's Chile: The Political Economy of the Rise and Fall of*

the Unidad Popular (New York: Cambridge University Press, 1976), pp. 32–40; Paul E. Sigmund, *The Overthrow of Allende and the Politics of Chile, 1964–1976* (Pittsburgh: University of Pittsburgh Press, 1977), chaps. 6 and 7; Arturo Valenzuela, *The Breakdown of Democratic Regimes: Chile* (Baltimore: Johns Hopkins University Press, 1978), chap. 3.

2. On the history of agrarian reform in Chile and the role of Frei's government in promoting it, see Robert R. Kaufman, *The Politics of Land Reform in Chile, 1950–1970: Public Policy, Political Institutions, and Social Change* (Cambridge: Harvard University Press, 1972). For other accounts of Frei's "Revolution in Liberty," see Paul Sigmund, *The Overthrow of Allende and the Politics of Chile,* chap. 3; Stefan de Vylder, *Allende's Chile,* chap. 1.

3. A constitutional amendment nationalizing the copper mines was unanimously adopted by Congress on July 11, 1971. See Paul Sigmund, *The Overthrow of Allende and the Politics of Chile,* p. 141. For Frei's "Chileanization" policies, see Markos Mamalakis and Clark Reynolds, *Essays on the Chilean Economy* (Homewood, Illinois: Irwin, 1965); Theodore Moran, *Multinational Corporations and the Politics of Dependence: Copper in Chile* (Princeton: Princeton University Press, 1974), chap. 4.

4. For an excellent analysis of the various political groups and their positions toward reform and democracy at the time of the presidential elections of 1970, see Arturo Valenzuela, *The Breakdown of Democratic Regimes: Chile,* pp. 39–49.

5. On Chilean democracy, see Frederico Gil, *The Political System of Chile* (Boston: Houghton Mifflin, 1966).

6. For the results of the 1970 presidential elections, see Paul A. Sigmund, *The Overthrow of Allende and the Politics of Chile,* pp. 106–12; Arturo Valenzuela, *The Breakdown of Democratic Regimes: Chile,* pp. 39–45.

7. According to the Constitution of 1925, if no candidate had obtained more than half of the valid votes, fifty days after the election a joint session of both houses of Congress was to decide between the two candidates with the highest proportion of votes. See Paul Sigmund, *The Overthrow of Allende and the Politics of Chile,* p. 96.

8. The parties of the extreme right—National Party and Patria y Libertad—would never vote for Allende.

9. For a detailed account of the several conspiracies to prevent Allende's accession to the presidency and of the role of U.S. corporations and the U.S. government in those conspiracies, see Paul Sigmund, *The Overthrow of Allende and the Politics of Chile,* pp. 112–27.

10. See Arturo Valenzuela, *The Breakdown of Democratic Regimes: Chile,* p. 48.

11. Ibid., p. 49.

12. On the abduction and assassination of General Schneider, see Paul Sigmund, *The Overthrow of Allende and the Politics of Chile,* pp. 120–23.

13. See Arturo Valenzuela, *The Breakdown of Democratic Regimes: Chile,* p. 49.

14. See Paul Sigmund, *The Overthrow of Allende and the Politics of Chile,* pp. 118–20.

15. On the fears of the Christian Democrats, see Arturo Valenzuela, *The Breakdown of Democratic Regimes: Chile,* pp. 70–77.

16. Robert R. Kaufman, *The Politics of Land Reform in Chile,* p. 98.

17. Paul Sigmund, *The Overthrow of Allende and the Politics of Chile,* p. 124.

18. Ibid. For a brief survey of Frei's redistributive policies, see William Ascher, *Scheming for the Poor: The Politics of Redistribution in Latin America* (Cambridge: Harvard University Press, 1984), pp. 121–47.

19. See Stefan de Vylder, *Allende's Chile,* chap. 6; Paul Sigmund, *The Overthrow of Allende and the Politics of Chile,* pp. 45–50, 80–84.

20. Only the minority at the extreme right was opposed to reform. Right-wing politicians were critical even of Frei's more moderate program of reforms. They characterized Frei as the Chilean Kerensky, claiming that he had paved the road for a Marxist takeover. See Paul Sigmund, *The Overthrow of Allende and the Politics of Chile,* p. 126. See also note 4 above.

21. For a description of Allende's position relative to the other groups in the Popular Unity coalition, see Arturo Valenzuela, *The Breakdown of Democratic Regimes: Chile,* p. 47.

22. On the Chilean Communist Party, see Ernst Halperin, *Nationalism and Communism in Chile* (Cambridge: MIT Press, 1965). For the moderation of the Communist Party during Allende's government, see Paul Sigmund, *The Overthrow of Allende and the Politics of Chile,* chaps. 7 and 8; Arturo Valenzuela, *The Breakdown of Democratic Regimes: Chile,* chaps. 2 and 3.

23. On the Socialist Party, see Salomom Corbalan, *El Partido Socialista* (Santiago: Imprensa Atenea, 1957); Julio Cesar Jobet, *El Partido Socialista de Chile* (Ediciones Prensa Latinoamericana, 1971). For the relations between radical Socialists and the MIR, see Arturo Valenzuela, *The Breakdown of Democratic Regimes: Chile,* pp. 45, 67–68, 79, 101.

24. The Movimiento de Accion Popular Unitario (MAPU) was formed on May 18, 1970, by a group of Christian Democratic dissidents who were dissatisfied with the pace of reforms under the Frei administration.

25. On the position of the Christian Democrats, see Paul E. Sigmund, "Christian Democracy in Chile," *Journal of International Affairs* 20 (1966): 332–42; Paul E. Sigmund, ed., *The Ideologies of the Developing Nations* (New York: Praeger, 1967), pp. 383–404; George Grayson, *El Partido Democrata Cristiano* (Buenos Aires: Francisco de Aguirre, 1968); Leonard Gross, *The Last Best Hope: Eduardo Frei and Chilean Christian Democracy* (New York: Random House, 1967); Arpad Von Lazar and Luiz Quiroz Varela, "Chilean Christian Democracy: Lessons in the Politics of Reform Management," *Inter-American Economic Affairs* 21 (1968): 51–72.

26. For the divisions within the Christian Democratic Party, see Paul Sigmund, *The Overthrow of Allende and the Politics of Chile,* pp. 118–20, 134–36.

27. See Arturo Valenzuela, *The Breakdown of Democratic Regimes: Chile,* p. 48.

28. See Paul Sigmund, *The Overthrow of Allende and the Politics of Chile,* pp. 133–34.

29. For the economic program and performance of the Popular Unity government, see Stefan de Vylder, *Allende's Chile;* Barbara Stallings, *Class Conflict and Economic Development in Chile* (Berkeley: University of California Press, 1978).

30. Stefan de Vylder, *Allende's Chile,* p. 145.

31. Paul E. Sigmund, *The Overthrow of Allende and the Politics of Chile,* p. 134.

32. See Arturo Valenzuela, *The Breakdown of Democratic Regimes: Chile,* p. 53.

33. Stefan de Vylder, *Allende's Chile,* p. 54.

34. For the debate around the effects of the cutbacks in international aid and credit on the performance of the Chilean economy under Allende's government, see Arturo Valenzuela, *The Breakdown of Democratic Regimes: Chile,* p. 56.

35. See William Ascher, *Scheming for the Poor* (Cambridge: Harvard University Press, 1984), pp. 250–51.

36. Arturo Valenzuela, *The Breakdown of Democratic Regimes: Chile,* p. 55.

37. Ibid.

38. Ibid., p. 56.

39. Paul Sigmund, *The Overthrow of Allende and the Politics of Chile,* pp. 162–64.

40. See Arturo Valenzuela, *The Breakdown of Democratic Regimes: Chile,* p. 61.

41. On the fear and reaction of the Christian Democrats, see Paul E. Sigmund, *The Overthrow of Allende and the Politics of Chile,* pp. 134–

60, esp. pp. 159–60; Arturo Valenzuela, *The Breakdown of Democratic Regimes: Chile,* pp. 70–80.

42. On the violent activities of the extremists of the left, see Arturo Valenzuela, *The Breakdown of Democratic Regimes: Chile,* p. 53; Paul Sigmund, *The Overthrow of Allende and the Politics of Chile,* pp. 139–40, 148–49.

43. For Allende's and the moderate leftists' positions on the violent activities of the radicals, as well as on their reluctance to repress or exclude them, see Arturo Valenzuela, *The Breakdown of Democratic Regimes: Chile,* pp. 67–68.

44. See note 42.

45. See Paul E. Sigmund, *The Overthrow of Allende and the Politics of Chile,* pp. 164–69.

46. Ibid., p. 158.

47. For the attempts of the government to gain control of the Alessandri paper company and the Christian Democrats' reaction, see ibid., pp. 157–58.

48. Ibid., p. 159.

49. On Allende's proposal, see ibid.

50. For the Christian Democratic proposal for a constitutional amendment regulating state control over the economy, see Arturo Valenzuela, *The Breakdown of Democratic Regimes: Chile,* p. 59; Paul E. Sigmund, *The Overthrow of Allende and the Politics of Chile,* pp. 159–60.

51. For an account of the events around the passage of the constitutional amendment, see Paul E. Sigmund, *The Overthrow of Allende and the Politics of Chile,* pp. 167–69.

52. On the political impasse created by the passage of the constitutional amendment on the three areas of the economy, see Arturo Valenzuela, *The Breakdown of Democratic Regimes: Chile,* pp. 73–80.

53. See ibid., pp. 76–77.

54. At that point in time neither side thought that the democratic regime was in danger. Lacking foresight, both sides did not hesitate to engage in confrontational tactics to win short-term victories. They failed to recognize the risks of confrontation and were ultimately the victims of their own actions. See ibid., p. 77.

55. For a detailed account of the talks, see ibid., p. 74.

56. See ibid.

57. See ibid.

58. On the second round of talks, see ibid., pp. 75–77.

59. Ibid., pp. 76–77.

60. On the role of the military in Chile, see Frederick M. Nunn, *The Military in Chilean Politics* (Albuquerque: University of New Mexico Press, 1970); Roy A. Hansen, "Military Culture and Organizational De-

cline: A Study of the Chilean Army," Ph.D. diss. (UCLA, 1968); Alain Joxe, *Las Fuerzas Militares en Chile* (Editorial Universitaria, 1970).

61. For an account of the politicization of the Chilean military, see Paul E. Sigmund, *The Overthrow of Allende and the Politics of Chile,* chap. 9.

62. For an account of the growing mobilization and confrontation during the second half of 1972, see Arturo Valenzuela, *The Breakdown of Democratic Regimes: Chile,* pp. 77–80.

63. On the involvement of the *gremios,* see Paul Sigmund, *The Overthrow of Allende and the Politics of Chile,* p. 150; Arturo Valenzuela, *The Breakdown of Democratic Regimes: Chile,* p. 78.

64. Paul Sigmund, *The Overthrow of Allende and the Politics of Chile,* p. 186.

65. For the activities of the government and the extreme left mentioned below, see Arturo Valenzuela, *The Breakdown of Democratic Regimes: Chile,* p. 79.

66. For an account of the appointment of General Prats and a description of his role in the Allende government, see Paul E. Sigmund, *The Overthrow of Allende and the Politics of Chile,* chap. 9.

67. On the 1973 congressional elections, see ibid., pp. 198–201; Arturo Valenzuela, *The Breakdown of Democratic Regimes: Chile,* pp. 83–87.

68. On the division of the military, Prats's resignation, and the forming of a new cabinet, see Arturo Valenzuela, *The Breakdown of Democratic Regimes: Chile,* pp. 88–90.

69. On the ENU, see Paul Sigmund, *The Overthrow of Allende and the Politics of Chile,* pp. 202–6.

70. See Arturo Valenzuela, *The Breakdown of Democratic Regimes: Chile,* p. 90.

71. See ibid., p. 92.

72. Ibid., p. 93.

73. Ibid.

74. For details on the coup of June 29, 1973, see Paul E. Sigmund, *The Overthrow of Allende and the Politics of Chile,* pp. 212–15.

75. See Arturo Valenzuela, *The Breakdown of Democratic Regimes: Chile,* pp. 100–101.

76. For the military's fear that the government and the radicals were organizing a "parallel army" and inciting the troops to disobedience, as well as for the raids the armed forces organized against the left, see ibid., pp. 101–2.

77. For Allende's belated attempt to reach an agreement with the Christian Democrats, see Paul Sigmund, *The Overthrow of Allende and the Politics of Chile,* pp. 218–25; Arturo Valenzuela, *The Breakdown of Democratic Regimes: Chile,* pp. 93–98.

78. For details on the formation of the "national security" cabinet, see Paul Sigmund, *The Overthrow of Allende and the Politics of Chile,* pp. 225–30.

79. Allende really broke with the radicals in his party. See Arturo Valenzuela, *The Breakdown of Democratic Regimes: Chile,* p. 103.

80. On the intransigence of the Christian Democrats and the events that followed, see ibid., pp. 103–6.

BIBLIOGRAPHY

Ames, Barry. *Political Survival: Politicians and Public Policy in Latin America*. Berkeley: University of California Press, 1987.

Anscombe, G. E. M. *Intention*. Oxford: Basil Blackwell, 1957.

Ascher, William. *Scheming for the Poor: The Politics of Redistribution in Latin America*. Cambridge: Harvard University Press, 1984.

Axelrod, Robert. *The Evolution of Cooperation*. New York: Basic Books, 1984.

Bandeira, Muniz. *O Govêrno João Goulart*. Rio de Janeiro: Civilização Brasileira, 1978.

Barnes, Julian. *Flaubert's Parrot*. London: Picador, 1985.

Barry, Brian. *Sociologists, Economists, and Democracy*. Chicago: University of Chicago Press, 1978.

Bastos, Elide R. *As Ligas Camponesas*. Petrópolis: Vozes, 1984.

Bates, Robert H. *Essays on the Political Economy of Rural Africa*. Berkeley: University of California Press, 1987.

Becker, Gary. *The Economic Approach to Human Behavior*. Chicago: University of Chicago Press, 1976.

Bem, D. "An Experimental Analysis of Self-Persuasion." *Journal of Experimental Social Psychology* 1 (1965): 199–218.

———. "Self-Perception: An Alternative Interpretation of Cognitive Dissonance Phenomena." *Psychological Review* 74 (1967): 183–200.

———. "Self-Perception Theory." *Advances in Experimental Social Psychology* 6 (1972): 1–62.

Benevides, Maria Victoria de Mesquita. *O PTB e o Trabalhismo: Partido e Sindicato em São Paulo, 1945–1964*. São Paulo: Brasiliense, 1989.

———. *A UDN e o Udenismo: Ambiguidades do Liberalismo Brasileiro (1945–1965)*. Rio de Janeiro: Paz e Terra, 1981.

Blanning, T. C. W. *The French Revolution: Aristocrats versus Bourgeois?* London, 1988.

Block, Fred. *Revising State Theory: Essays in Politics and Postindustrialism*. Philadelphia: Temple University Press, 1987.

Boudon, Raymond. *The Unintended Consequences of Social Action*. New York: St. Martin's Press, 1981.

Bowles, S., and Herbert Gintis. *Schooling in Capitalist America*. London: Routledge and Kegan Paul, 1976.

Brams, Steven J. *Game Theory and Politics*. New York: Free Press, 1975.

———. *Paradoxes in Politics*. New York: Free Press, 1976.

Branco, Carlos Castelo. *Introdução à Revolução de 1964*. Vol. 1. Rio de Janeiro: Artenova, 1975.

Camargo, Aspasia. "A Questão Agrária: Crise de Poder e Reformas de Base (1930–1964)." In *História Geral da Civilização Brasileira*. Tomo III, vol. 3. São Paulo: Difel, 1977.

Cardoso, Fernando H. "Associated Dependent Development: Theoretical and Practical Implications." In *Authoritarian Brazil*, ed. Alfred Stepan. New Haven: Yale University Press, 1973.

Carnoy, Martin. *The State and Political Theory*. Princeton: Princeton University Press, 1984.

Carone, Edgar. *O P.C.B. (1943–1964)*. São Paulo: Difel, 1982.

Charlton, William. *Weakness of Will: A Philosophical Introduction*. New York: Basil Blackwell, 1988.

Chilcote, Ronald H. *The Brazilian Communist Party: Conflict and Integration, 1922–1972*. New York: Oxford University Press, 1974.

Cobban, Alfred A. *The Social Interpretation of the French Revolution*. Cambridge: Cambridge University Press, 1964.

Cohen, G. A. "Functional Explanation, Consequence Explanation, and Marxism." *Inquiry* 25 (1982): 27–56.

Cohen, Youssef. "The Benevolent Leviathan: Political Consciousness among Urban Workers under State Corporatism." *American Political Science Review* 76 (1982): 46–59.

———. "Democracy from Above: The Political Origins of Military Dictatorship in Brazil." *World Politics* 40 (1987): 30–50.

———. "The Heresthetics of Coup Making." *Comparative Political Studies* 24 (1991): 344–64.

———. "The Impact of Bureaucratic-Authoritarian Rule on Economic Growth." *Comparative Political Studies* 18 (1985): 123–36.

———. *The Manipulation of Consent: The State and Working-Class Consciousness in Brazil*. Pittsburgh: University of Pittsburgh Press, 1989.

Collier, David, ed. *The New Authoritarianism in Latin America*. Princeton: Princeton University Press, 1979.

Comminel, G. *Rethinking the French Revolution: Marxism and the Revisionist Challenge*. London, 1987.

Cook, K. S., and M. Levi. *The Limits of Rationality*. Chicago: University of Chicago Press, 1990.

Corbalan, Salomon. *El Partido Socialista*. Santiago: Imprensa Atenea, 1957.

Coser, Lewis. "Social Conflict and the Theory of Social Change." In *Conflict Resolution: Contributions of the Behavioral Sciences*, ed. C. G. Smith. Notre Dame: University of Notre Dame Press, 1971.

Costa, Sergio A. *O CGT e as Lutas Sindicais Brasileiras (1960–1964).* São Paulo: Grêmio Politécnico, 1981.

Daland, Robert T. *Brazilian Planning: Development Politics and Administration.* Chapel Hill: University of North Carolina Press, 1967.

Dallmayr, F. R., and T. A. McCarthy, eds. *Understanding and Social Inquiry.* Notre Dame: University of Notre Dame Press, 1977.

D'Araujo, Maria Celina Soares. *O Segundo Govêrno Vargas, 1950–1954.* Rio de Janeiro: Zahar, 1982.

Davidson, Donald. *Essays on Actions and Events.* New York: Oxford University Press, 1980.

———. "Paradoxes of Irrationality." In *Philosophical Essays on Freud,* ed. R. Wolheim and J. Hopkins. Cambridge: Cambridge University Press, 1982.

Delgado, Lucilia de Almeida Neves. *O Comando Geral dos Trabalhadores, 1961–1964.* Petrópolis: Vozes, 1986.

———. *PTB: Do Getulismo ao Reformismo (1945–1964).* São Paulo: Marco Zero, 1989.

De Souza, Amaury. "The Nature of Corporative Representation: Leaders and Members of Organized Labor in Brazil." Ph.D. dissertation, Massachusetts Institute of Technology, 1978.

De Souza, Maria do Carmo Campello de. *Estado e Partidos Políticos no Brasil.* São Paulo: Editora Alfa-Ômega, 1976.

De Vylder, Stefan. *Allende's Chile: The Political Economy of the Rise and Fall of the Unidad Popular.* Cambridge: Cambridge University Press, 1976.

Dos Santos, Wanderley G. "Autoritarismo e Após: Convergências e Divergências entre Brasil e Chile." *Dados* 25 (1982): 151–63.

———. "The Calculus of Conflict: Impasse in Brazilian Politics and the Crisis of 1964." Ph.D. dissertation, Stanford University, 1979.

Doyle, William. *Origins of the French Revolution.* Oxford: Oxford University Press, 1980.

———. *The Oxford History of the French Revolution.* Oxford: Oxford University Press, 1990.

Dray, W. H. *Laws and Explanation in History.* Oxford: Oxford University Press, 1957.

Dreifuss, René A. *1964: A Conquista do Estado.* Petrópolis: Vozes, 1981.

Dunn, Robert. *The Possibility of Weakness of Will.* Indianapolis: Hackett, 1987.

Elster, Jon. *The Cement of Society.* Cambridge: Cambridge University Press, 1989.

———. *Explaining Technical Change.* Cambridge: Cambridge University Press, 1982.

———. "Introduction." In *Rational Choice,* ed. Jon Elster. New York: New York University Press, 1986.

———. *Making Sense of Marx*. Cambridge: Cambridge University Press, 1985.

———. "Marxism, Functionalism, and Game Theory." *Theory and Society* 11 (1982): 453–82.

———. *Nuts and Bolts for the Social Sciences*. Cambridge: Cambridge University Press, 1989.

———. *Sour Grapes*. Cambridge. Cambridge University Press, 1985.

———. *Ulysses and the Sirens: Studies in Rationality and Irrationality.* Cambridge: Cambridge University Press, 1979.

Erickson, Kenneth P. *The Brazilian Corporative State and Working-Class Politics*. Berkeley: University of California Press, 1977.

Erickson, Kenneth P., and Patrick V. Peppe. "Dependent Capitalist Development, U.S. Foreign Policy, and Repression of the Working Class in Chile and Brazil." *Latin American Perspectives* 3 (1976): 19–44.

Evans, Peter. *Dependent Development.* Princeton: Princeton University Press, 1979.

Figueiredo, Argelina M. C. "Political Coalitions in Brazil, 1961–1964: Alternatives to Political Crisis." Ph.D. dissertation, University of Chicago, 1987.

Filho, Luiz V. *O Govêrno Castelo Branco*. Rio: José Olympio, 1975.

Fingarette, H. *Self-Deception.* London: Routledge and Kegan Paul, 1969.

Fishlow, Albert. "Some Reflections on Post-1964 Brazilian Economic Policy." In *Authoritarian Brazil,* ed. Alfred Stepan. New Haven: Yale University Press, 1973.

Fitch, John S. *The Military Coup d'Etat as a Political Process: Ecuador, 1948–1966*. Baltimore: Johns Hopkins University Press, 1977.

Flynn, Peter. *Brazil: A Political Analysis*. Boulder: Westview Press, 1983.

Foster, John. *Class Struggle and the Industrial Revolution.* London: Methuen, 1974.

Franco, Afonso Arinos de Melo. *Evolução da Crise Brasileira.* São Paulo: Editora Nacional, 1965.

Friedman, J. "A Noncooperative Equilibrium for Supergames." *Review of Economic Studies* 38 (1971): 1–12.

Friedman, Milton. "The Methodology of Positive Economics." In *Essays in Positive Economics,* ed. Milton Friedman. Chicago: University of Chicago Press, 1953.

Fudenberg, D., and E. Maskin. "The Folk Theorem in Repeated Games with Discounting or with Incomplete Information." *Econometrica* 54 (1986): 533–54.

Furet, François. *Interpreting the French Revolution.* Cambridge: Cambridge University Press, 1981.

Furtado, Celso. *Análise do Modêlo Brasileiro*. Rio de Janeiro: Civilização Brasileira, 1972.

———. "Political Obstacles to the Economic Development of Brazil." In *Obstacles to Change in Latin America,* ed. Claudio Veliz. London: Oxford University Press, 1965.

Geddes, Barbara. "A Game Theoretic Model of Reform in Latin American Democracies." *American Political Science Review* 85 (June 1991): 371–92.

Gil, Frederico. *The Political System of Chile*. Boston: Houghton Mifflin, 1966.

Gold, D., C. Lo, and E. O. Wright. "Recent Developments in Marxist Theories of the State." *Monthly Review* 27 (1975): 29–51.

Grayson, George. *El Partido Democrata Cristiano*. Buenos Aires: Francisco de Aguirre, 1968.

Gross, Leonard. *The Last Best Hope: Eduardo Frei and Chilean Christian Democracy*. New York: Random House, 1967.

Halperin, Ernst. *Nationalism and Communism in Chile*. Cambridge: MIT Press, 1965.

Hansen, Roy A. "Military Culture and Organizational Decline: A Study of the Chilean Army." Ph.D. dissertation, University of California, Los Angeles, 1968.

Hardin, Russell. *Collective Action*. Baltimore: Johns Hopkins University Press, 1982.

———. "Rationality, Irrationality, and Functional Explanation." *Social Science Information* 19 (1980): 775–82.

Harding, Timothy F. "The Political History of Organized Labor in Brazil." Ph.D. dissertation, Stanford University, 1973.

Harsanyi, J. C. "Advances in Understanding Rational Behavior." In *Rational Choice,* ed. Jon Elster. New York: New York University Press, 1986.

———. "Rational-Choice Models of Political Behavior vs. Functionalist and Conformist Theories." *World Politics* 21 (1969): 513–38.

Harvey, J., and G. Weary. "Current Issues in Attribution Theory and Research." *Annual Review of Psychology* 35 (1984): 427–59.

Hayek, F. A. *The Counter-Revolution of Science: Studies on the Abuse of Reason*. Glencoe: Free Press, 1952.

Hecter, Michael. "Comment: On the Inadequacy of Game Theory for the Solution of Real-World Collective Action Problems." In *The Limits of Rationality,* ed. Cook and Levi. Chicago: University of Chicago Press, 1990.

Hippólito, Lúcia. *De Rapôsas e Reformistas: O PSD e a Experiência Democrática Brasileira (1945–1964)*. Rio de Janeiro: Paz e Terra, 1985.

Hirschman, Albert O. "The Political Economy of Import-Substituting

Industrialization in Latin America." In *A Bias for Hope,* ed. A. O. Hirschman. New Haven: Yale University Press, 1971.

———. *Rival Views of Market Society.* New York: Viking, 1986.

———. "The Social and Political Matrix of Inflation: Elaborations on the Latin American Experience." In *Essays in Trespassing: Economics to Politics and Beyond,* ed. A. O. Hirschman. Cambridge: Cambridge University Press, 1980.

———. "The Turn to Authoritarianism in Latin America and the Search for Its Economic Determinants." In *The New Authoritarianism in Latin America,* ed. David Collier. Princeton: Princeton University Press, 1979.

Hobsbawm, E. J. *Echoes of the Marseillaise: Two Centuries Look Back on the French Revolution.* New Brunswick: Rutgers University Press, 1990.

Horowitz, Irving L., and Ellen K. Trimberger. "State Power and Military Nationalism in Latin America." *Comparative Politics* 8 (1976): 223–44.

Humphrey, John. *Capitalist Control and Workers' Struggle in the Brazilian Auto Industry.* Princeton: Princeton University Press, 1982.

Hunt, Lynn. *Politics, Culture, and Class in the French Revolution.* Berkeley: University of California Press, 1984.

Jaguaribe, Hélio. *Condições Institucionais do Desenvolvimento Brasileiro.* Rio de Janeiro: ISEB, 1958.

Jessop, Bob. *Theories of the State.* New York: New York University Press, 1983.

Jobet, Julio Cesar. *El Partido Socialista de Chile.* Ediciones Prensa Latinoamericana, 1971.

Joxe, Alain. *Las Fuerzas Militares en Chile.* Editorial Universitaria, 1970.

Jurema, Abelardo. *Sexta-Feira 13: Os Últimos Dias do Govêrno João Goulart.* Rio de Janeiro: Ed. O Cruzeiro, 1964.

Kahneman, D., P. Slovic, and A. Tversky, eds. *Judgement under Uncertainty.* Cambridge: Cambridge University Press, 1982.

Kaufman, Robert. "Industrial Change and Authoritarian Rule in Latin America: A Concrete Review of the Bureaucratic-Authoritarian Model." In *The New Authoritarianism in Latin America,* ed. David Collier. Princeton: Princeton University Press, 1979.

———. *The Politics of Land Reform in Chile, 1950–1970: Public Policy, Political Institutions, and Social Change.* Cambridge: Harvard University Press, 1972.

Kreps, David M. *A Course in Microeconomic Theory.* Princeton: Princeton University Press, 1990.

Labaki, A. *1961: A Crise de Renúncia e a Solução Parlamentarista.* São Paulo: Brasiliense, 1986.

Levi, Margaret. *Of Rule and Revenue.* Berkeley: University of California Press, 1988.

Linz, Juan J. *The Breakdown of Democratic Regimes: Crisis, Breakdown, and Reequilibration.* Baltimore: Johns Hopkins University Press, 1979.

Lloyd, Christopher. *Explanation in Social History.* New York: Basil Blackwell, 1986.

Luce, R. D., and H. Raiffa. *Games and Decisions.* New York: Wiley, 1957.

Lukes, Steven. "Methodological Individualism Reconsidered." In *Sociological Theory and Philosophical Analysis,* ed. Dorothy Emmet and Alasdair MacIntyre. New York: MacMillan, 1970.

MacIntyre, Alasdair. "The Idea of a Social Science." In *Against the Self-Images of the Age,* ed. Alasdair MacIntyre. New York: Schocken, 1971.

Malinowski, Bronislaw. *Magic, Science, and Religion.* Boston: Beacon Press, 1948.

Mamalakis, Markos, and Clark Reynolds. *Essays on the Chilean Economy.* Homewood, Illinois: Irwin, 1965.

Marini, Rui M. *Dialéctica de la Dependencia.* Mexico City: Nueva Era, 1973.

———. *Subdesarollo y Revolución.* Mexico City: Siglo Vientiuno, 1969.

Marx, Karl. *The Eighteenth Brumaire of Louis Bonaparte.* New York: International Publishers, 1963.

McDonough, Peter J. *Power and Ideology in Brazil.* Princeton: Princeton University Press, 1981.

Mele, Alfred R. *Irrationality: An Essay on Akrasia, Self-Deception, and Self-Control.* Oxford: Oxford University Press, 1987.

Mericle, Kenneth S. "Conflict Regulation in the Brazilian Industrial Relations System." Ph.D. dissertation, University of Wisconsin, 1974.

Merton, Robert K. "Manifest and Latent Functions." In *On Theoretical Sociology,* ed. Robert K. Merton. New York: Free Press, 1967.

Meyerson, Roger G. *Game Theory: Analysis of Conflict.* Cambridge: Harvard University Press, 1991.

Miliband, Ralph. "The Capitalist State: Reply to Nicos Poulantzas." *New Left Review* (1970) 59.

———. "Poulantzas and the Capitalist State." *New Left Review* 92 (1973): 83–92.

———. *The State in Capitalist Society.* New York: Basic Books, 1969.

Miller, D., and M. Ross. "Self-Serving Biases in the Attribution of Causality: Fact or Fiction?" *Psychological Bulletin* 82 (1975): 213–35.

Moon, Donald J. "The Logic of Political Inquiry: A Synthesis of Opposed Perspectives." In *Handbook of Political Science, Volume 1,* ed.

Fred I. Greenstein and Nelson Polsby. Reading, Mass.: Addison-Wesley, 1975.

Moran, Theodore. *Multinational Corporations and the Politics of Dependence: Copper in Chile.* Princeton: Princeton University Press, 1974.

Morley, Samuel A., and Gordon W. Smith. "The Effects of Changes in the Distribution of Income on Labor, Foreign Investment, and Growth in Brazil." In *Authoritarian Brazil,* ed. Alfred Stepan. New Haven: Yale University Press, 1973.

Nisbett, Richard, and Lee Ross. *Human Inference: Strategies and Shortcomings of Social Judgement.* Englewood Cliffs: Prentice-Hall, 1980.

Nordlinger, Eric A. *Soldiers in Politics: Military Coups and Governments.* Englewood Cliffs: Prentice-Hall, 1977.

Nunn, Frederick M. *The Military in Chilean Poltics.* Albuquerque: University of New Mexico Press, 1970.

O'Brien, Philip, ed. *Allende's Chile.* New York: Praeger, 1976.

O'Connor, James. *The Fiscal Crisis of the State.* New York: St. Martin's Press, 1973.

O'Donnell, Guillermo A. "Corporatism and the Question of the State." In *Authoritarianism and Corporatism in Latin America,* ed. James M. Malloy. Pittsburgh: University of Pittsburgh Press, 1977.

———. *Modernization and Bureaucratic-Authoritarianism.* Berkeley: Institute of International Studies, University of California, 1973.

———. "Reflections on the Patterns of Change in the Bureaucratic-Authoritarian State." *Latin American Research Review* 13 (1978): 3–38.

———. "Tensions in the Bureaucratic-Authoritarian State and the Question of Democracy." In *The New Authoritarianism in Latin America,* ed. David Collier. Princeton: Princeton University Press, 1979.

Offe, Claus. "The Capitalist State and the Problem of Policy Formation." In *Stress and Contradiction in Modern Capitalism,* ed. L. N. Lindberg et al. Lexington: D. C. Heath, 1973.

———. "Structural Problems of the Capitalist State: Class Rule and the Political System. On the Selectiveness of Political Institutions." In *German Political Studies,* ed. Klaus Von Bayme. Beverly Hills: Sage, 1974.

———. "Theses on the Theory of the State." *New German Critique* 6 (1975): 137–47.

Olson, Mancur. *The Logic of Collective Action.* Cambridge: Harvard University Press, 1965.

Ordeshook, Peter C. *Game Theory and Political Theory: An Introduction.* Cambridge: Cambridge University Press, 1986.

Paige, Jeffrey M. *Agrarian Revolution: Social Movements and Export*

Agriculture in the Underdeveloped World. New York: Free Press, 1975.

Pears, David. *Motivated Irrationality.* Oxford: Oxford University Press, 1984.

Pion-Berlin, David. "Political Repression and Economic Doctrines." *Comparative Political Studies* 16 (1983): 37–66.

Popper, Karl R. *The Open Society and Its Enemies.* London: Routledge and Kegan Paul, 1945.

———. *The Poverty of Historicism.* London: Routledge and Kegan Paul, 1957.

Poulantzas, Nicos. *Classes in Contemporary Capitalism.* London: New Left Books, 1975.

———. *Fascism and Dictatorship.* London: New Left Books, 1974.

———. *Political Power and Social Classes.* London: New Left Books, 1974.

———. "The Problem of the Capitalist State." *New Left Review* 58 (1969): 67–78.

Przeworski, Adam. *Capitalism and Social Democracy.* Cambridge: Cambridge University Press, 1985.

———. "Marxism and Rational Choice." *Politics and Society* 14 (1985): 379–409.

Rabinow, P., and W. M. Sullivan, eds. *Interpretive Social Science: A Reader.* Berkeley: University of California Press, 1979.

Riker, William H., and Peter C. Ordeshook. *An Introduction to Positive Political Theory.* Englewood Cliffs: Prentice-Hall, 1973.

Rodrigues, José A. *Sindicato e Desenvolvimento no Brasil.* São Paulo: Difel, 1968.

Rodrigues, Leôncio Martins. *Conflito Industrial e Sindicalismo no Brasil.* São Paulo: Difel, 1966.

———. "O PCB: Os Dirigentes e a Organização." In *História Geral da Civilização Brasileira.* Tomo III, Vol. 3. São Paulo: Difel, 1977.

Sartori, Giovanni. "European Political Parties: The Case of Polarized Pluralism." In *Political Parties and Political Development,* ed. Joseph LaPalombara and Myron Weiner. Princeton: Princeton University Press, 1966.

———. *Parties and Party Systems: A Framework for Analysis.* Cambridge: Cambridge University Press, 1976.

Schama, Simon. *Citizens: A Chronicle of the French Revolution.* New York: Knopf, 1989.

Schilling, Paulo R. *Como se Coloca a Direita no Poder.* Vol. 1. São Paulo: Global, 1979.

Schmitter, Philippe C. *Interest Conflict and Political Change in Brazil.* Palo Alto: Stanford University Press, 1968.

Schneider, Ronald M. *The Political System of Brazil: Emergence of a*

Modernizing Authoritarian Regime. New York: Columbia University Press, 1971.

Schwartzman, Simon. *São Paulo e o Estado Nacional.* São Paulo: Difel, 1975.

Sen, A. K. "Behavior and the Concept of Preference." In *Rational Choice,* ed. Jon Elster. New York: New York University Press, 1986.

———. "Choice Functions and Revealed Preferences." *Review of Economic Studies* 38 (1971).

Serra, José. "Three Mistaken Theses Regarding the Connection between Industrialization and Authoritarian Regimes." In *The New Authoritarianism in Latin America,* ed. David Collier. Princeton: Princeton University Press, 1979.

Sheehan, John. "Market-Oriented Economic Policies and Political Repression in Latin America." *Economic Development and Cultural Change* 28 (1980): 264–89.

Shubik, Martin. *Game Theory in the Social Sciences: Concepts and Solutions.* Cambridge: MIT Press, 1984.

Sigmund, Paul E. "Christian Democracy in Chile." *Journal of International Affairs* 20 (1966): 332–42.

———. *The Overthrow of Allende and the Politics of Chile, 1964–1976.* Pittsburgh: University of Pittsburgh Press, 1977.

Sigmund, Paul E., ed. *The Ideologies of the Developing Nations.* New York: Praeger, 1967.

Skidmore, Thomas E. *Politics in Brazil, 1930–1964: An Experiment in Democracy.* New York: Oxford University Press, 1967.

———. "Politics and Economic Policy Making in Authoritarian Brazil, 1937–1971." In *Authoritarian Brazil,* ed. Alfred Stepan. New Haven: Yale University Press, 1973.

———. "The Politics of Economic Stabilization in Postwar Latin America." In *Authoritarianism and Corporatism in Latin America,* ed. James M. Malloy. Pittsburgh: University of Pittsburgh Press, 1977.

Skocpol, Theda. "Bringing the State Back In: Strategies of Analysis in Current Research." In *Bringing the State Back In,* ed. Peter B. Evans, D. Rueschemeyer, and Theda Skocpol. Cambridge: Cambridge University Press, 1985.

———. *States and Social Revolutions: A Comparative Analysis of France, Russia, and China.* Cambridge: Cambridge University Press, 1979.

———. *Vision and Method in Historical Sociology.* Cambridge: Cambridge University Press, 1984.

Soares, Gláucio A. D. *Sociedade e Política no Brasil.* São Paulo: Difel, 1973.

Stallings, Barbara. *Class Conflict and Economic Development in Chile*. Berkeley: University of California Press, 1978.

Stepan, Alfred. *The Military in Politics: Changing Patterns in Brazil*. Princeton: Princeton University Press, 1971.

———. "Political Leadership and Regime Breakdown: Brazil." In *The Breakdown of Democratic Regimes*, ed. Juan J. Linz and Alfred Stepan. Baltimore: Johns Hopkins University Press, 1978.

———. *The State and Society: Peru in Comparative Perspective*. Princeton: Princeton University Press, 1978.

Stephens, J., E. H. Stephens, and D. Reuschemeyer. *Capitalist Development and Democracy*. Chicago: University of Chicago Press, 1992.

Stinchcombe, Arthur L. *Constructing Social Theories*. New York: Harcourt, Brace, and World, 1968.

———. "Is the Prisoner's Dilemma All of Sociology?" *Inquiry* 23 (1980): 187–92.

———. "Merton's Theory of Social Structure." In *The Idea of a Social Structure: Papers in Honor of Robert Merton*, ed. Lewis Coser. New York: Harcourt Brace Jovanovich, 1974.

Swift, Jeannine. *Agrarian Reform in Chile*. Lexington: D. C. Heath, 1971.

Taylor, G. V. "Noncapitalist Wealth and the Origins of the French Revolution." *American Historical Review* 79 (1967): 469–96.

Taylor, Michael. *Anarchy and Cooperation*. London: Wiley, 1976.

———. *Community, Anarchy, and Liberty*. Cambridge: Cambridge University Press, 1982.

———. *The Possibility of Cooperation*. Cambridge: Cambridge University Press, 1987.

———. "Rationality and Revolutionary Collective Action." In *Rationality and Revolution*, ed. Michael Taylor. Cambridge: Cambridge University Press, 1988.

Tilly, Charles. "Revolutions and Collective Violence." In *Handbook of Political Science*, ed. F. I. Greenstein and N. W. Polsby. Reading: Addison-Wesley, 1975.

Therborn, Goran. *What Does the Ruling Class Do When It Rules?* London: New Left Books, 1978.

Thompson, E. P. "The Moral Economy of the English Crowd in the Eighteenth Century." *Past and Present* 50 (1971).

Toledo, Caio N. *O Govêrno Goulart e o Golpe de 64*. São Paulo: Brasiliense, 1982.

Trimberger, Ellen K. *Revolution from Above*. New Brunswick, N.J.: Transaction Books, 1978.

Tsebelis, George. *Nested Games: Rational Choice in Comparative Politics*. Berkeley: University of California Press, 1990.

Valenzuela, Arturo. *The Breakdown of Democratic Regimes: Chile.* Baltimore: Johns Hopkins University Press, 1978.

Valenzuela, Arturo, and J. Samuel Valenzuela, eds. *Chile: Politics and Society.* New Brunswick: Transaction, 1976.

Viana, Cíbilis da Rocha. *Reformas de Base e a Política Nacionalista de Desenvolvimento—De Getúlio a Jango.* Rio de Janeiro: Civilização Brasileira, 1980.

Viana, Luiz W. *Liberalismo e Sindicato no Brasil.* Rio: Paz e Terra, 1976.

Vinhas, Moisés. *O Partidão: A Luta por um Partido de Massas, 1922–1974.* São Paulo: Hucitec, 1982.

Von Lazar, Arpad, and Luiz Quiroz Varela. "Chilean Christian Democracy: Lessons in the Politics of Reform Management." *Inter-American Economic Affairs* 21 (1968): 51–72.

Von Wright, G. H. *Explanation and Understanding.* Ithaca: Cornell University Press, 1971.

Wallerstein, Michael. "The Collapse of Democracy in Brazil." *Latin American Research Review* 15 (1980): 3–40.

Weffort, Francisco. *O Populismo na Política Brasileira.* São Paulo: Paz e Terra, 1980.

Winch, Peter. *The Idea of a Social Science and Its Relation to Philosophy.* London: Routledge and Kegan Paul, 1958.

———. "Understanding a Primitive Society." *American Philosophical Quarterly* 1 (1964): 307–24.

Wrong, Dennis. "The Oversocialized Conception of Man in Modern Sociology." *American Sociological Review* 26 (1961): 183–93.

Zammit, Ann, ed. *The Chilean Way to Socialism.* Austin: University of Texas Press, 1973.

INDEX